CULTS AND ISMS

CULTS AND ISMS

Twenty Alternates

to

Evangelical Christianity

by

Russell P. Spittler

BAKER BOOK HOUSE
Grand Rapids, Michigan

Library of Congress Catalog Card Number: 62-21702

Copyright, 1962, by
BAKER BOOK HOUSE

ISBN: 0-8010-7980-2

First printing, December 1962
Second printing, July 1966
Third printing, March 1968
Fourth printing, July 1970
Fifth printing, January 1973
Sixth printing, September 1973
Seventh printing, August 1974
Eighth printing, August 1975

PHOTOLITHOPRINTED BY CUSHING - MALLOY, INC.
ANN ARBOR, MICHIGAN, UNITED STATES OF AMERICA
1975

DEDICATED
to those who are seeking the Truth
and
to those who have been found by Him

Preface

I never cease to be amazed at the variety and vitality of religious societies spawned by the seeking heart. Without the controls of written revelation and driven by understandable inner demands for spiritual realities, many men and many movements have peeled away from the evangelical center of Christianity and now populate its fringe. A number of these constitute the "Third Force"—a term popularized by Henry P. Van Dusen, who was thinking of historic Protestantism on the one hand and Roman Catholicism on the other.

In this small volume twenty movements of varying distances from the evangelical center of Christianity are surveyed. The general pattern followed in each case had been to outline briefly both the history and distinctive teachings of the group, then to provide a compact evaluation from an evangelical standpoint. The book is, therefore, intended to supply the evangelical Christian with a brief but adequate survey of the major American cults.

It is always a problem in studies of this sort to know whether or not to include Roman Catholicism and what has been rather poorly called "modernism." Warranting as they do far more detailed critiques than are manageable here, they are included as necessary to any survey of "alternates to evangelical Christianity."

I wish it to be transparently clear that I do not impugn the person of any devotee of any group here discussed. One of the lingering results of my study of the cults has been a heightened sense of the sincerity and dedication of their adherents. I cannot be convinced that it is Christian either to ridicule or to curse the sincere searchings of any religious person, however distant he may be from evangelical Christianity. There are, I know, "doctrines of devils." And there is an obligation laid on the Christian to speak for the truth—which is why I wrote this book. But polemic controversy cannot come near the evangelistic potential of simply holding high the saving facts about the Person of the Man of Calvary, accompanied by the penetrating power of the convincing Spirit.

In the attempt to fairly represent the beliefs of these groups, I have in most instances been able to use materials secured from the groups themselves. I shall be most grateful, incidentally, to any who would do me the courtesy of pointing out errors of fact or interpretation. It is a pleasure to acknowledge dependence upon other writers in this field, most notably Horton Davies, John H. Gerstner, Walter R. Martin, and J. K. Van Baalen.

This book originated as a manual prepared for the church schools of the Assemblies of God. The opportunity to make it more widely available in this enlarged and revised form I owe to the generosity of the Gospel Publishing House, Springfield, Missouri.

The outlined format of the original work has been retained in order to facilitate use of the book as a text, not only in local church study groups (for which inexpensive matching Student Manuals may be secured from the Gospel Publishing House, Springfield, Missouri), but also for theological schools and colleges and even for home study.

I wish to thank especially my wife Bobbie for her consistent understanding and encouragement, and Miss Dorothy Knott for her careful preparation of the typescript.

May the God of all truth bring us all to the unity of the faith that is focused in His Son.

Russell P. Spittler

Central Bible Institute
Springfield, Missouri
July, 1962

Contents

CHAPTER I

Introducing the Cults

This is a religious world. More than 75 per cent of the world's population adhere to one of five major world religions—Christianity, Mohammedanism, Hinduism, Confucianism, or Buddhism. In the United States there are more than 250 religious bodies. Above 63 per cent of all Americans belong to some religious group.

A growing segment of American religion is commonly called the non-Christian cults. There are a half-dozen or so major ones and an endless array of smaller ones, some of passing interest, some of surprising endurance. The majority of these "cults"—which they must be called for lack of a more suitable word—unwittingly merge into what a *Life* magazine article termed "The Third Force in Christendom" (June 9, 1958). This third force looms as a challenging though instructive alternative to Roman Catholicism and Protestantism.

An understanding of the historical backgrounds and major teachings of these groups is imperative for an effective and aggressive Christian witness. This book has been developed specifically to trace the principal forms of religion regarded by evangelical Christianity as theologically defective or spiritually inadequate.

But before we can study the cults, we must first know what a cult is. How does a cult differ from a sect or from a church or denomination? How does growth of cults compare with that of the larger Christian bodies? What attitude should we have toward the cults and toward individual members of them? What is the best way to present the claims of Christ to one who is a member of a cult? Questions concerning cults may be compressed into a series of four questions which easily outline this initial chapter.

WHAT IS A CULT?

Just what is a *cult*? How do we define the term, so we can decide who belongs to a cult and who does not? This is a complex question, made more so by the curious fact that words have emotional stingers as well as dictionary definitions.

Definition

From the dictionary we get an authoritative definition of a *cult*: "A system of worship of a deity . . . the rites of a religion . . . great devotion to some person, idea, or thing, especially such devotion viewed as an intellectual fad . . . a sect." This tells us right away that a cult is devoted to some teaching and that it has religious aspects.

Let us now see how textbook writers define the word. Hear first Walter R. Martin, an evangelical writer in this field: "By cultism we mean the adherence to doctrines which are pointedly contradictory to orthodox Christianity and which yet claim the distinction of either tracing their origin to orthodox sources or of being in essential harmony with those sources. Cultism, in short, is any major deviation from orthodox Christianity relative to the cardinal doctrines of the Christian faith."[1]

Notice the lack of an absolute standard of reference, such as Walter Martin's definition gives to "orthodox Christianity," in the following definition. It comes from a careful scholar, Charles S. Braden, who unapologetically remains an "unrepentant liberal": "A cult, as I define it, is any religious group which differs significantly in some one or more respects as to belief or practice from those religious groups which are regarded as the normative expressions of religion in our total culture."[2]

A *cult* then is any group that claims to be Christian but falls short of an evangelical definition of Christianity. This definition does not suit every movement discussed in this book, but it explains the omission of the major world religions and the inclusion of Roman Catholicism and Modernism.

Contrast

If this is a *cult*, what is a *sect*? The words are often used interchangeably. Quite often, even generally, either word is used in a derogatory sense to express contempt toward minority religious groups.

William W. Sweet, a Methodist church historian, offers a suggestive distinction: "A *cult* is a religious group which looks for its

---

[1]*The Rise of the Cults* (Grand Rapids: Zondervan Publishing House, 1955), p. 12.

[2]*These Also Believe* (New York: The Macmillan Company, 1949), p. 12.

basic and peculiar authority outside the Christian tradition."[3] While most cults pretend to be correctly interpreting the Bible, they usually have high regard for some other literature without which the Bible cannot properly be understood.

For example, each of the following cults accepts the authority of the Bible, or so they say. Yet each also insists upon the use of the listed materials as a necessary aid to interpreting the Bible:

Cult	Non-Biblical Source of Authority
Christian Science	*Science and Health, with Key to the Scriptures*
Mormonism	*Book of Mormon*
Jehovah's Witnesses	Writings of G. T. Russell and J. F. Rutherford
Unity	Writings of Charles and Myrtle Fillmore
Swedenborgianism	Writings of Emanuel Swedenborg

A *sect* is closer to traditional Christianity than a cult. A church, when contrasted with a sect, appears larger, older, and more concerned with collective religious action than with personal conversion. Sects, Dr. Sweet points out, often grow into churches. He uses his own church, the Methodist, as a key example of this pattern.

HOW DO THE CULTS THREATEN THE CHURCH?

Why study the cults? We do not expect to expand our theology by what we learn there. Why not let the cults be about their own business while we go about ours? Why not preach a positive gospel and forget about the cults?

Here are some significant ways the cults affect the life and work of the church—ways which demand the straight-forward attention of the church.

By Proselyting

One of the disturbing features of the challenge of the cults is their evangelistic program—if we may misapply a phrase. The editors of *Christianity Today* lament, "It is significant that they first approach known Christians. Seldom do they attempt to reach the unevangelized, which should be the first step in any genuine missionary program."[4]

It appears that the happy hunting grounds of the cult propagandist is the discontented Christian, one who is a nominal member of a Christian church but who has had no personal redemptive ex-

---

[3]*American Culture and Religion* (Dallas: Southern Methodist University Press, 1951), p. 92.

[4]Harold Lindsell, *et al.*, *The Challenge of the Cults* (Grand Rapids: Zondervan Publishing House, 1961), p. 74.

perience. Because his deep inner needs go unsatisfied, he falls prey to the novelty and superficial satisfactions advertised by the cults. This, of course, calls to court the lethargy of the Christian church and not the least potential benefit of a fresh study of the cults may be a summons to exchange creed-guarding for grace-dispensing in the message and mission of the church.

By Falsely Emphasizing the Bible

Most cults do not oppose the Bible: they claim to unfold it. Follow them, we hear promised, and they will lead us down enlightening paths beside the not-so-still waters of fantastic Biblical exposition.

To provide this guidance, of course, demands some sort of interpreter who will show us the way. The Bible, one must come to believe if he heeds the cults, cannot be interpreted by the open mind standing in obedience before open Scripture and beneath a God "that revealeth secrets." So each cult has its "Wayshower," its enlightening literature.

That the cults generally uphold rather than devalue the Bible is doubly dangerous because of the deep-seated respect for the Bible in American culture. The writer once led Bible studies at a reformatory for teen-age girls. Guilty of every imaginable teen-age crime (and of some unimaginable), these girls yet showed profound respect for the Bible as the Word of God. There is enough of the Christian heritage left in the rapidly secularizing American culture to presume that most people, unless they have been educated out of the belief, have high respect for the Bible even though they neither know nor obey it. Accordingly, when a cultist proposes to interpret the Bible he is building on a ready-made foundation.

By Spreading Doctrinal Error

This error-by-error tour through the theology of the cults will disclose to the reader a multitude of beliefs contrary to those held by the consensus of believing Christian churches. Where the church witnesses to a Living God who is Three-in-One, the cults proclaim either One or Three. Where the church teaches resurrection, the cults offer reincarnation. Where the church announces salvation by grace, the cults outline salvation by works.

Such a din of many doctrinal voices in the world complicates the task of the church in teaching the true doctrines of the faith to a spiritually sleepy world.

By Rapid Growth

"Are the Cults Outpacing Our Churches?" asked Harold Lindsell in the opening chapter of *The Challenge of the Cults*. His answer is surprising—no. The average growth rate of a selected group of cults between the years 1950 and 1960 he calculated to be from 30 to 35 per cent. During the same years, the average for all religious bodies was right at 33 per cent. What these percentages do not reveal, of course, is numerical increase. In the period cited, for example, the Mormons added 366,000—a 30 per cent increase; while the Presbyterian bodies, at a 20 per cent rate, added over twice as many—740,000.

One thing is clear: The cults are at least equalling the growth rate of the churches—and this in spite of the fact that a cult convert must agree to be added to the roster.

WHY ARE THE CULTS THRIVING?

To be a good Mormon, you would have to believe that God the Father has a body of flesh and bones similar to yours. As a Theosophist, you would point to "love at first sight" as evidence that the couple knew each other in a previous life before this reincarnation. As a Christian Scientist, you would say the "other Comforter" Jesus promised came in the form of "Divine Science." To an evangelical Christian these ideas are not only blasphemous, they are ridiculous. Why then are the groups that sponsor them growing?

Because They Meet Human Needs

You cannot deny this. The writer once probed two Mormon missionaries—both promising, intelligent young men—to see if they were sons of their church or converts to it. They were converts— both from a well-known Christian denomination, both within the previous five years. Then I asked, amazed that they should shift from traditional Christianity to such a group, "What attracted you to Mormonism?" One said, "Everything came together for me." He found doctrinal satisfaction. The other said, "I used to have nothing to live for; I saw no meaning in life. Now I have a cause to believe in." He found personal fulfillment.

I could not question the sincerity of these men. They must have found something in their cult for them to have gone so far away from the Christian faith. The only answer is that they felt they had had their needs met.

But you say, "These people are hopelessly blinded by Satan:

that's why they follow the cults." And I say, "See how Satan blinds them—by meeting their needs."

The logic is sobering. Can the church afford not to meet the needs, the physical needs of people? Did not Jesus channel the healing of the body into the healing of the soul? Did the Good Samaritan first meet a physical or a spiritual need? Did not the early church enroll the widows in order to minister to their needs? Let the church be reminded that "meeting needs" is a method, not a motto.

Because They Are Aggressive

The Mormons take first place here. Two by two, their young men systematically cover the whole city—without regard for their lives in this or that house. Morman missionaries rush in where Christian personal workers fear to tread. They remind one of what God said to Ezekiel: "And they, whether they will hear, or whether they will forbear, (for they are a rebellious house,) yet shall know that there hath been a prophet among them" (Ezekiel 2:5). But this is from the Christian Bible. Is there any reason Christian aggressiveness should not equal or exceed Mormon persistence?

Because They Are Authoritative

They have been persuaded. They genuinely believe in the gospel offered by the cult. They are sold on what they sell. They have been trained in set patterns of presenting their message and of answering objections. They have not worked out these patterns for themselves. They follow standard operating procedures. They use the Bible convincingly. They come prepared and practiced. They come upon one not expecting a theological debate and unequipped if he were. Such persons are then easily impressed with the authoritativeness of the cult propagandist.

And somehow, men are built with an interior demand for outside authority. They want someone to tell them what to do, what to believe, what is right, what is wrong. If they can locate such a definite and detailed authority, it takes away the burden of thinking for themselves.

It is really not so unnatural after all. Jesus insists He be the Lord of every life—the last Source of authority. If men reject Him as Lord ("and . . . no man can say that Jesus is the Lord, but by the Holy Ghost"), they will usually find some other authority.

WHAT IS THE BEST WAY TO APPROACH A CULTIST?

Shall we burst into their meetings with an avalanche of quoted Scripture? Shall we insult them, ridicule their distinctives? Or shall we avoid them, let them live their own lives as we do ours? Is there a list of Scripture passages which can be memorized that will refute all cults, or maybe a course we can take that will assure triumph in debate? Here are a few specific suggestions for dealing with such people:

Do Not Argue

And do not ridicule. It is quite possible to win an argument and lose a soul. And it is equally possible, through the convicting power of the Holy Spirit of God, to lose an argument and win a soul. Paul advises Timothy to be a good servant of the Lord by "instructing those that oppose themselves," showing that error demands the loving care of a concerned guardian rather than the gloating triumph of the argumentative gladiator. This passage of Scripture is instructive. It continues, "If God peradventure will give them repentance to the acknowledging of the truth; and that they may recover themselves out of the snare of the devil, who are taken captive by him at his will" (II Timothy 2:25, 26).

Testify

A delicate skill in tactfully pointing out error in a cultist's system is a lingering need, and one that can be improved through study. But an even more powerful weapon is a simple personal testimony, "Here's what God did for me." Nothing can replace the old-fashioned testimony, provided it has up-to-date freshness and is a true *testimony*—a report of God's action in your life and not merely a pious "vain repetition."

Exalt Christ

The point of any testimony should be the impact of Christ on the life of the individual. Jesus was really talking about His impending crucifixion when He said, "And I, if I be lifted up from the earth, will draw all men unto me" (John 12:32). But His drawing power only began then: it continues as men, in their testimonies, decrease, and He increases.

Get the Facts

Do not accuse a Mormon of practicing polygamy today. They excommunicate anyone they find adopting the practice. (They do, however, still insist polygamy is a higher law, which they forego wherever the law of the land forbids the practice.) Do not accuse a Roman Catholic of being prohibited from reading the Bible. To avoid errors like this, one must study, as you are now doing.

Stress Fulfillment

In working with cultists, "agree with thine adversary quickly." Start with what is common ground. Recognize that he accepted the teachings of the cult because they had some value for him. But move on from here to show how Christ fulfills to an immeasurably greater degree the goals he seeks. And show that there is only one way to Jesus—through the Cross.

FOR DISCUSSION

1. How would you answer each of the main division questions in this lesson?
2. Should the church be concerned with human needs other than spiritual?
3. What is good and what is bad about argument and testimony as methods?

CHAPTER II

Saints Alive—in Utah

Mormonism

It may happen to you. A knock on the door announces two neatly dressed young men who ease their way into your living room. They explain they are from the Church of Jesus Christ and say they wish to share their testimony with you.

In a few minutes, you will have learned how the ancient inhabitants got to America, how Christ appeared to them after His resurrection, and how God miraculously called Joseph Smith to restore the apostate church with the aid of *The Book of Mormon* miraculously translated from golden plates over a hundred years ago and since taken back by the delivering angel.

These clean-cut young men are missionaries of the Church of Jesus Christ of Latter Day Saints, with imposing headquarters in Salt Lake City, Utah. They are "Mormons"—a nickname for Latter Day Saints not officially adopted by the church and derived from *The Book of Mormon* which they recognize as inspired revelation just like the Bible.

Largest of the cults, Mormonism has grown with increasing speed to a world-wide membership now approaching two million. It began in 1830 with six members.

Mormonism has a fascinating history indelibly stamped upon the westward push of the American frontier. Its theology is exceedingly complex, and an unbelievably immense mass of literature has been produced by, for, and against the Mormons.

HISTORY

Palmyra, New York

Joseph Smith, Jr., the Prophet. Born on December 22, 1805, Joseph Smith moved with his poverty-stricken parents and nine other children to New York. Stirred by revivalistic preaching, young Joseph—he was about fifteen—was deeply disturbed over the bickering among various denominations. Reading James 1:5, he began to pray in an effort to learn which was right.

"Revelations." In 1820—at age fourteen—he saw a vision: "I saw two Personages, whose brightness and glory defy all description, standing above me in the air. One of them spake unto me, calling me by name, and said, pointing to the other—*This is My Beloved Son. Hear Him!"*[1] In 1823 the angel Moroni appeared to Joseph Smith and disclosed to him the location of a partially buried box containing golden plates in the "reformed Egyptian tongue," together with "two stones in silver bows" for translating the plates.

The Book of Mormon. Not until 1827 was Joseph directed to remove the plates from their place in the Hill Cumorah near Palmyra. Taking three years to translate the book by dictating through a curtain, Joseph finally published *The Book of Mormon* in 1829. The angel then recovered the plates, and they are no longer to be seen. Many passages of *The Book of Mormon* are identical to the King James Version, published over two hundred years earlier.[2] For this reason, the reports about the discovery of *The Book of Mormon* are not generally believed by any but Mormons.

Founding of the Church. The next year, on April 6, 1830, in the town of Fayette in Seneca county the Church of Jesus Christ was organized. Joseph was designated "a seer, a translator, a prophet, an Apostle of Jesus Christ," and was made the ruler of the church. He was twenty-four years old.

Kirtland, Ohio

When persecution evicted the tiny church from New York, its members fled to Kirtland on Lake Erie, their headquarters from 1831 to 1837. Consolidation and growth took place, and they erected a large temple. Completed in 1836, this temple still stands. It is now owned by the Reorganized branch of the Latter Day Saints.

Zion, Missouri

By 1831, missions had already been sent from Kirtland to Missouri. Here Joseph Smith dedicated the plot of ground upon which Mormons still believe a great temple will be erected. Located in

---

[1] See the interesting and brief autobiography (only a dozen pages long) found in *The Pearl of a Great Price* (Salt Lake City: The Church of Jesus Christ of Latter-Day Saints, 1952), pp. 46–58.

[2] Arthur Budvarson documents with photographic reproductions a negative answer to the question which titles his book, *The Book of Mormon—True or False?* (Grand Rapids: Zondervan Publishing House, 1961).

Independence, Missouri, the temple lot is shared by three separate groups giving allegiance to Joseph Smith as their founder. Through hostile persecution and finally governmental force, the Mormons were pushed out of Missouri.

Nauvoo, Illinois

Arriving on the swampy banks of the Mississippi forty-five miles north of Quincy, Illinois, the Mormon settlers by 1844 had erected a complete city of twenty thousand inhabitants. Joseph Smith was mayor, and the Mormons became a significant political force in Illinois. In 1844 Joseph Smith was nominated (by the Mormons) as a candidate for the presidency of the United States. A million-dollar temple was erected, which was later destroyed. While in the jail at Carthage, Illinois, awaiting trial over the Mormon confiscation of an anti-Mormon newspaper, irate citizens stormed the building and murdered the prophet and his brother Hyrum. This martyrdom, while it was followed by a brief period of confusion and disorganization, became a rallying point for the Mormons. Their leader had died for his faith.

Salt Lake City, Utah

The Westward Trek. Two years after the death of the prophet-founder, Mormon forces rallied and began a pioneer trek to a land whose identity they knew not. In covered wagons, later with small pushcarts, they moved 1500 miles into the far west which was then part of Mexico.

Brigham Young. The one who rose to provide leadership after the exodus from Nauvoo was the brilliant colonist Brigham Young. It was he, not Joseph Smith, who led the "Rocky Mountain Saints" to Salt Lake. Rejecting his leadership, a group of Mormons in 1860 formed the Reorganized Church of Jesus Christ of Latter Day Saints. This group rejects plural marriage and has other important differences.

Current Status. Twelve exclusive temples (non-Mormons may not enter[3]), a vast relief society that provides for the poor, Brigham Young University with 10,000 students—these are but a few facets of the Mormon empire.

---

[3]What more than a million visitors to Salt Lake City see each year is the Mormon *Tabernacle*, which is immediately adjacent to the Temple—where even the *Mormons* gain entrance only by proper permission.

DOCTRINES

Sources of Authority

Description. Of utmost importance in any religious system is the accepted standard of doctrine. The wide variation in world religions and even in Christian denominations may be traced to the holy books and creeds received by each group. What are the accepted sacred books of Mormonism? They number four:

1. *The Bible.* "We believe the Bible to be the word of God as far as it is translated correctly," states the "Articles of Faith," section eight. Joseph Smith began a revision of the King James Version that is sometimes called the "Inspired Version." "However, since the work was never finished, the Church has accepted the King James translation as its standard English text of the Bible."[4]

2. *The Book of Mormon.* The eighth article of faith quoted above continues, "We also believe the Book of Mormon to be the word of God." This book professes to be an account of the original inhabitants of America, to whom Christ appeared following His resurrection (an appearance not mentioned by Paul in his list found in I Corinthians 15:4-8). It was originally written in "reformed Egyptian characters"—a language unknown to scholarship —and translated through the aid of two miraculous stones.

3. *The Doctrine and Covenants.* This is a record of 136 "revelations" by which the Bible has been expanded. The Reorganized Church does not accept the "revelation" authorizing polygamy, and the Church of Christ, Temple Lot, reduces the book still further and uses the older title, *The Book of Commandments.*

4. *The Pearl of a Great Price.* Usually bound together with *The Doctrine and Covenants,* this volume contains "The Book of Moses" (suspiciously close to Genesis), a "Book of Abraham" claiming to have been written by himself, a translation by and a partial history of Joseph Smith, and the brief, one-page "Articles of Faith."

Response. When Mormons attribute to the writings of fellow Mormons authority equal to the Bible, they forget that Scripture never began with man. God's Spirit moved first. As He inspired men to speak or write, the words of those men were actually the Word of God. But God started the process (II Peter 1:21).

In His providence, God gave the church the books he intended to constitute the Bible. He allowed no room for additional "inspired writing." It is significant that a curse on those who add to or

---

[4]Gordon B. Hinckley, *What of the Mormons:* (5th ed. rev.; Salt Lake City: The Church of Jesus Christ of Latter-Day Saints, 1954), p. 100.

take away from God's Word appears, not only throughout the Bible (Deuteronomy 4:2; 12:32; Proverbs 30:6), but also at the end of the Book of Revelation (22:18, 19)—the end of the Bible itself.

Curious Ideas about God

Description. "We believe in God, the Eternal Father, and in His Son, Jesus Christ, and in the Holy Ghost"—so reads the first Article of Faith. But the explanation of this belief as found throughout Mormon writings clearly shows an unorthodox understanding of this article. One of Joseph Smith's "revelations" brought the following description of the Father: "The Father has a body of flesh and bones as tangible as man's."[5] Reads the *Book of Moses,* 6:9, "In the image of his own body, male and female, created he them. . . ." "Even in bodily appearance the Father and the Son are alike."[6] No one can view the Father as possessing an actual physical body and believe in the Christian conception of the Trinity. The unity of the three persons is, in Mormon theology, a unity of purpose and power only and not a unity of substance and essence.

Response. The Greek original behind John 4:24—"God is a spirit"—puts the word *spirit* first, the position used for emphasis. The little word *a* is omitted in Greek. The definite article *the* occurs in front of *God,* stressing identity. This is the ordinary construction in Greek used to tell the quality of something. The verse clearly tells that God is of spirit-quality. Place this fact beside Luke 24:39, "A spirit hath not flesh and bones," and the Mormon theology is demolished if we are to employ right methods of interpretation. While it does well to recognize the threeness of the Godhead, Mormonism too little appreciates the essential unity of the Godhead.

Curious Ideas about God

Description. The virgin birth does not appear as a prominent plank in Mormon theology. Talmage's *Articles of Faith,* widely used standard interpretation of Joseph Smith's original "articles," has little to say about this doctrine. Walter Martin has preserved a quotation from Brigham Young:

> When the Virgin Mary conceived the Child Jesus, the Father had begotten him in his own likeness. He was *not* begotten by the Holy Ghost. And who

---

[5]*The Doctrines and Covenants,* 130:22 (Salt Lake City: The Church of Jesus Christ of Latter-Day Saints, 1952), p. 238.

[6]James E. Talmage, *Articles of Faith* (42nd ed.; Salt Lake City: The Church of Jesus Christ of Latter-Day Saints, 1961), p. 41

was the Father? He was the first of the human family. . . . Jesus, our elder brother, was begotten in the flesh by the same character that was in the garden of Eden, and who is our Father in Heaven.[7]

Response. This quotation will reach the nostrils of any true Christian as a blasphemous stench. It contradicts flatly the record of Jesus' miraculous birth of a virgin recorded in Luke 1:26-38. Yet as Dr. Martin points out, the Mormons deceptively answer "yes" to the question, "Do Mormons believe in the virgin birth?" in an article appearing in *Look* magazine for October 5, 1954.

Sin and Salvation

Description. "Sin is any condition, whether omission of things required or in commission of acts forbidden, that tends to prevent or hinder the development of the human soul."[8] Mormons feel that it was both necessary and appropriate for Adam to sin, since he thereby brought about the possibility of becoming as God: "It has become a common practice with mankind to heap reproaches upon the progenitors of the family, and to picture the supposedly blessed state in which we would be living but for the fall; whereas our first parents are entitled to our deepest gratitude for their legacy to posterity—the means of winning title to glory, exaltation, and eternal lives."[9]

Mormons prefer the term *exaltation* to *salvation.* Their goal is perfection, to become even as God. This is achieved by taking best advantage of the time allowed to each man on earth. What he gains here determines his status there. Heaven is a place having three levels, each one ministered to by a member of the Godhead—the sphere ruled by the Father being most desirable. Punishment for sin is not endless.

Response. The Christian understanding of sin reaches beyond acts, or their absence, into the nature of fallen man (Romans 5:12). Since the Fall, man has been in total rebellion against God. The only deliverance from this downward pull is that effected by God Himself in the vicarious atonement of Jesus Christ (Acts 4:12). Mormons lack an understanding of grace.

Celestial Marriage and Plural Marriages

Description. Mormons take God's command to "be fruitful, and multiply" literally. Unless prohibited for physical reasons or other-

---

[7]Brigham Young, *Journal of Discourses,* Vol. 1, pp. 50, 51. Quoted by Walter R. Martin, *Mormonism* (2nd ed. rev.; Grand Rapids: Zondervan Publishing House, 1960), p. 26.
[8]Talmage, *op. cit.,* p. 56.
[9]*Ibid.,* p. 70.

wise, they are required to marry and produce offspring. Worthy Mormons whose commitment to the church is unquestioned are permitted the rite of celestial marriage executed only in one of the sacred temples. This rite seals a marriage, which ordinarily is a contract for duration of life only, as an eternal marriage. Persons thus sealed have their marriages solemnized forever—even after death.

Plural marriage, sometimes called polygamy, has been widely connected with the Mormons. Contrary to popular opinion, Mormons do not now practice polygamy in the United States and their church has officially opposed its practice since 1890. Excommunication is the penalty for any found practicing plural marriage.

But while Mormons do not practice plural marriage, they still believe it is God's highest law. Since they endeavor to be good citizens (and no one familiar with them can deny this), and since the federal laws forbid the practice of plural marriage, they refrain from its practice.

One of the major differences between the Utah Mormons and the Reorganized Church is the latter's rejection of polygamy. It is their claim that *The Book of Mormon* itself does not permit polygamy (Jacob 2:27). And they omit from *The Doctrine and Covenants* the "revelation" (Section 132, Utah edition) introducing this practice, holding that this section was never produced by Joseph Smith—who elsewhere, as they claim, denies the practice. Utah Mormons believe plural marriage will be restored after the Second Coming.[10]

Response. The apostle Paul once escaped a council by pitting the Pharisees against the Sadducees (Acts 23:1-10). Orthodox Christians may profit from the writings of the Reorganized Church against the Utah Mormons on the topic of plural marriage. Both churches claim Joseph Smith as their founder. But which is correct about his teaching on plural marriage? The Mormon concept of "celestial marriage" teaches that a man will live with his wife in eternity just as he lives with her during this life; and Mormons believe reproduction will continue during eternity. Jesus taught the Sadducees differently: "For in the resurrection they [humans] neither marry, nor are given in marriage, but are as the angels of God in heaven" (Matthew 22:30).

As for plural marriage, whether in practice or in belief, the apostle Paul declared that ministers and church leaders were to be

---

[10]Bruce McConkie, *Mormon Doctrine*, pp. 522, 523. Cited by Russell F. Ralston, *Fundamental Differences Between the Reorganized Church and the Church in Utah* (Independence, Missouri: Herald House, 1960), p. 87.

the husbands of one wife each (I Timothy 3:2, 12; Titus 1:6). The Mormon concept of plural marriage cannot be reconciled with Scripture.

Baptism for the Dead

Description. Mormons do not baptize infants, but they immerse (not in public ceremonies) converts. They appear to adopt the idea of baptismal regeneration, that the new birth transpires at the time of baptism. In the temples, members of the church may be baptized by proxy for those who died without accepting the teachings of Joseph Smith, such as the heathen who have not heard or ancestors who lived during the apostasy of the church before the Restoration led by Joseph Smith. Departed souls have another opportunity to hear the "gospel" which, according to Mormonism, will be preached to them in the spirit world. Since they cannot be baptized because they are without bodies, and since baptism is necessary for salvation, the living may serve the dead by being baptized in their stead.

Response. I Corinthians 15:29—". . . why are they then baptized for the dead?"—is the only Biblical references to this practice. The verse appears in a passage where Paul argues in favor of a literal resurrection of the body. But in referring to the obscure practice (it is not clear just what this verse means), Paul neither commands it nor approves it: he merely uses it to support his argument. Pointing to I Peter 3:18-20 and 4:6, Mormons assume the dead have an opportunity to hear the gospel. But the word for *preach* in these verses is used in the past tense. These difficult verses may be understood as a triumphant proclamation by Christ to the spirit world once and for all of the glorious victory He was about to achieve in the resurrection.

EVALUATION

1. *Mormons are good people.* No purpose is served in denying the many statistics and facts they produce to document their patriotism, citizenship, industry, and moral goodness. They care for one another with a welfare program rarely equalled by any other religious group. They can produce lists of illustrious Mormons—Ezra Taft Benson, former Secretary of Agriculture; Gene Fullmer, former middle-weight champion; George Romney, president of American Motors. And there are many other "fruits" by which we are expected to "know them." As a social group, the Mormons are exceptional.

2. *But there is a vast difference between human goodness and spiritual righteousness.* "All our righteousnesses are as filthy rags," claimed Isaiah (64:6). The lost dimension in the theology of Mormonism is grace. They do not rightly perceive that our standing with God is based, not on what we *do,* but on what Christ has *done.*

3. *The fundamental error of Mormonism is its acceptance of revelation outside the Bible.* The "revelations" comprising *The Doctrine and Covenants* will strike any Bible reader as petty and trivial, concerned with tiny things rather than with the loftier themes of the Bible. *The Book of Mormon* has to be accepted by a blind sort of "faith," and neither its original language nor its contents are recognized by responsible scholarship.

4. *The point of approach to Mormons should be the Bible.* "The Bible," Talmage reports of his church in his *Articles of Faith,* is "the foremost of her standard works, first among the books which have been proclaimed as her written guides in faith and doctrine."[11] The whole of Mormon theology is exceedingly complex, though readily accessible for firsthand study. As in dealing with any adherent of another religion, the Christian must be in prayer continually and evince a Christian spirit at all times. May God grant personal knowledge of the Truth—Jesus Christ Himself—to such as seek His face.

For Further Reading

Inexpensive missionary editions of the *Book of Mormon,* the *Doctrine and Covenants* (containing also the *Pearl of a Great Price*), and Talmage's *Articles of Faith* are readily available through Mormon churches and missionaries. Nothing replaces first-hand study of these volumes.

The Reorganized branch has clarified its less offensive position both in a full length book (*Fundamental Differences Between the Reorganized Church and the Church in Utah,* Herald House, 1960, by Russell F. Ralston) and in an inexpensive tract by Elbert A. Smith, *Differences that Persist.* Both may be had from Herald House, Box 447, Independence, Missouri.

G. B. Hinkley's *What of the Mormons,* though calculated to elicit sympathy, is an excellent brief summary of the status and history of the Utah Mormons. Typical of the hostile nineteenth-century denunciations of Mormonism is a scathing book with the amusing title *USA—Uncle Sam's Abscess,* which is author William Jarman's (he is an apostate Mormon) term for Mormonism. This work was published in England in 1884.

For evangelical Christian criticism, Walter R. Martin's full-length book is most ample: *The Maze of Mormonism* (Zondervan, 1962). There are also several pamphlets of use. The same Walter Martin wrote *Mormonism,*

---

[11]Talmage, *op. cit.,* p. 236.

a pamphlet in the Zondervan Modern Cult Library. William Biederwolf's *Mormonism Under the Searchlight* (Eerdman's, *n.d.*) is a bit out of date. Louis T. Talbot's *What's Wrong with Mormonism?* (Dunham, *n.d.*) has some value. The Utah Christian Mission, P.O. Box 1743, Phoenix, Arizona, publishes a variety of useful material for Christian workers wishing to reach Mormons.

For Discussion

1. Recount the facts pertaining to the discovery of *The Book of Mormon*.
2. Which are the standard sources of authority for Mormonism?
3. What is "celestial marriage"? Do Mormons practice polygamy?
4. Explain the reasoning behind the practice of baptizing for the dead.
5. Summarize briefly the leading theological errors of Mormonism.
6. Which is the fundamental error?

CHAPTER III

Sunday on Saturday

Seventh-Day Adventism

March 21, 1843—it was a day of great excitement. After much study a Baptist farmer had announced that the Lord would return on that day. Thousands confidently expected the Lord to break through the clouds at any moment.

But the day came and the day went.

The figures were checked; an error was discovered. The Lord was to come a year later. More excitement. Then disappointment again. Another recheck, and another date—October 22, 1844. But October 23 came and went as usual.

Out of this unfortunate date-setting experience has arisen what is known today as the Seventh-day Adventist movement—a million and a half strong around the world. Sincere in conviction, sacrificial in giving, ambitious in global missions—this church stands as a memorial to intense concern with the prophetic Word.

Seventh-day Adventists no longer believe in date-setting. Indeed, they never did. Recognizing the error of William Miller's announced date, they were nevertheless committed to the Adventist message. By reinterpretation, it was decided that Christ did come in 1844—only His "coming" was a transfer of heavenly location and shift of ministry.

Accepting the inspiration of the Bible, the Trinity, the deity and virgin birth of Christ and His vicarious atonement, Seventh-day Adventists present a puzzling picture to the student. For in addition to these evangelical truths they adopt some strange teachings. They themselves wish to be known as evangelicals—proclaimers of the true gospel message. While the degree to which conservative Christians accept them varies from voluntary defense to violent opposition, the distinctive doctrines of Seventh-day Adventism perpetuate their isolation.

HISTORY

William Miller

Baptist Farmer-preacher. One of the features of the religion of the American frontier was the variety of ministerial methods. The Presbyterians used well-trained pastors and concentrated on religious education, founding many colleges. The Methodists utilized the famed circuit rider with many "classes" under his care. The Baptists had many self-supporting men who farmed in the day and preached in the evenings and on Sundays. One such Baptist farmer-preacher was William Miller, who had come to Low Hampton, New York, from his birthplace—Pittsfield, Massachusetts.

Born in 1782, just a few years after America had achieved its independence, Miller had a devout mother but experienced an intense struggle with deism—a view of religion denying God's personal concern for the world He had created, a view popular during Revolutionary days and espoused by none less than Thomas Jefferson. However, William Miller was genuinely converted.

Prophetic Interpretation. After his conversion, Miller turned to a study of the Bible. He became interested in prophetic themes. In particular, the significance of the "two thousand and three hundred days" mentioned in Daniel 8:14 attracted him. Perhaps under the influence of Ezekiel 4:6 ("I have appointed thee each day for a year"), Miller took each "day" to refer to a year. This he did probably without knowing that the original Hebrew is more correctly translated (as in the American Standard Version) "two thousand and three hundred evenings and mornings."

Based on Daniel 9:25, the year 457 B.C. (the year the Persian king Artaxerxes permitted Ezra to spearhead a return to Jerusalem), was assumed to be the beginning of the 2300 years. Adding 2300 years to this date yields the year A.D. 1843. "I was thus brought," he reports in his own words preserved by modern writers, "in 1818 at the close of my two-year study of the Scriptures to the solemn conclusion that in about twenty-five years from that time all the affairs of our present state would be wound up."[1]

Enthusiastic Expectancy. With the date set for the return of the Lord, a quarter century of fervent preaching began. Miller published a pamphlet with the long but startling title *Evidence from Scripture and History of the Second Coming of Christ about the Year 1843.* Shortly, other publications arose: *The Signs of*

---

[1]Quoted by Francis D. Nichol, *The Midnight Cry* (Washington, D. C.: Review and Herald Publishing Association, 1944), p. 35.

the Times, in Boston; *The Midnight Cry,* in New York; and *The Philadelphia Alarm.* As the date approached interest increased, and so did Miller's followers. At the peak of excitement there were from 50,000 to 100,000 people confidently expecting the return of the Lord in 1843.

As the day approached closer and closer, preparations were made. Reports exist of people climbing upon housetops in appropriate garb, of some closing stores and breaking up homes, and even of cases of insanity and suicide. But these reports are convincingly denied by Adventist apologists and may be examples of imaginative expansion of rumors. But that there was an exciting spirit of expectancy, no one would deny.

"The Great Disappointment." The appointed day—March 21, 1843—came and went without the Lord's return. Some recalculation led to the conclusion that the figures were wrong by a year; the Lord would return March 21, 1844. Again, the day passed. Finally, certain Jewish manners of reckoning time produced the date of October 22, 1844.

Though William Miller was wrong, he was honest—a rare combination. Walter Martin preserves Miller's honest confession of error: "Were I to live my life over again, with the same evidence that I then had, to be honest with God and man I should have to do as I have done. . . . I confess my error, and acknowledge my disappointment; yet I still believe that the Day of the Lord is near, even at the door; and I exhort you, my brethren, to be watchful and not let that day come upon you unawares."[2] Concludes Dr. Martin: "I believe he now enjoys the presence of the Lord whose appearing he so anxiously awaited."[3]

Miller himself never was a Seventh-day Adventist. He never accepted the SDA teachings about the Sabbath, the investigative judgment, soul-sleep, and annihilation. He died in 1849.

The Triple Source of Seventh-day Adventism

Dr. Martin's researches have revealed a threefold source of the denomination now known as the Seventh-day Adventists. Each strand contributed some teaching to the movement. Here is a review of each.

1. *Hiram Edson: New York.* Dedicated disciples of William Miller, Hiram Edson and a friend plodded slowly and despondently

---

[2]S. Bliss, *Memoirs of William Miller,* p. 256. Quoted by Walter R. Martin, *The Truth About Seventh-day Adventism* (Grand Rapids: Zondervan Publishing House, 1960), p. 28.
[3]*Ibid.,* p. 30.

through a cornfield near Port Gibson, New York, the very next day after "the great disappointment." Daniel 8:14, the verse referring to the 2300 day-years, also adds, "Then shall the sanctuary be cleansed." Miller and his followers had assumed this "sanctuary" was the earth itself to which Christ would return. On this day in the cornfield, however, Hiram Edson suddenly received a vision disclosing that the "sanctuary" was not at all on earth, but in heaven itself. It occurred to him then, that while William Miller was correct in his date, he was incorrect about what took place on that date. At this time, so Edson discovered, Christ entered the heavenly sanctuary—not the earthly one, and so of course His "coming" was not visible, being rather a change of location in heaven. It is this reinterpretation that lies at the basis of current Seventh-day Adventist theology in its doctrine of the sanctuary cleansing and the investigative judgment.

2. *Joseph Bates: Massachusetts and New Hampshire.* A second group centering in two New England states and headed by a retired sea captain taught the necessity of observing Saturday as the unchangeable Sabbath. Support for this was found in Revelation 14:12, where the third angel speaks of "they that keep the commandments of God"—one of which was the Fourth Commandment regarding the Sabbath.

3. *Ellen G. White: Maine.* This group stressed the relevance of the gifts of the Spirit for the present age and recognized in Mrs. White the "spirit of prophecy." For that reason, the writings of Mrs. White are highly regarded to this day by Adventists.

Formation of Adventist Societies. After the great disappointment of 1844, a period of disorganization naturally occurred. By 1855, however, the three groups outlined above merged their numbers and their doctrines and set up headquarters at Battle Creek, Michigan. In 1860 the name *Seventh-day Adventist* was adopted officially, and in 1903 headquarters were transferred to Takoma Park, Washington, D.C. In 1861 the *Advent Christian Church* was formed. This second largest Adventist group worships on Sunday and considers itself less legalistic than the Seventh-day Adventists. Several other smaller groups formed, such as the *Life and Advent Union* in 1864.

Seventh-day Adventism Today

Statistics. In 1960 there were 317,852 baptized adult members distributed throughout 3,032 churches in the United States. Worldwide, there are some 1,150,000 members and a Sabbath school enrollment exceeding a million and a half. Forty-four publishing houses produce literature in 220 languages. On 860 stations and in 65 languages the Voice of Prophecy is broadcast regularly. In 1959 they ranked second (after the Free Methodists, at $243.95) in per-capita giving for all purposes, averaging gifts totaling $217.31 per member per year. They are noted for medical missions, having over 400 physicians in more than 200 medical units. Adventists, incidentally, do not use tobacco or alcoholic beverages.

Status. How evangelical are the Seventh-day Adventists? Admittedly the closest of the cults to evangelical Christianity, SDA (as the movement is commonly abbreviated) restated its beliefs with the publication in 1957 of a 700-page volume entitled *Questions on Doctrine.*[4] This volume leaves no doubt they wish to be considered evangelical.

Reaction to the volume among evangelicals varied. Men like Louis Talbot, M. R. DeHaan, and J. K. Van Baalen remain firm in repudiating any change for the better in SDA. On the other hand, Donald Grey Barnhouse and Walter Martin feel that SDA is basically evangelical but has a number of doctrines separating the movement from the evangelical church.

What shall be our attitude? It is only fair to judge the Adventists by the teachings they now embrace, considering carefully the historical development of their teachings. In this chapter *Questions on Doctrine* has been taken as an authoritative guide to current Adventist theology. It should not be overlooked, however, that at least two men—D. M. Canright and E. B. Jones—after long and distinguished service with the Adventists repudiated Adventist theology.

DOCTRINES

Seventh-day Adventists do believe in the unique inspiration of the Bible. They accept the full deity of Christ and believe He was born of a virgin and was physically and miraculously resurrected. They teach He died for our sins and that forgiveness comes by grace alone. They await the imminent return of the Lord. On these points, they are orthodox; and this is why some accept them as fundamentally orthodox.

But there are a number of other teachings unique to the SDA. There is space only to summarize them briefly.

---

[4]*Seventh-day Adventists Answer Questions on Doctrine: An Explanation of Certain Aspects of Seventh-day Adventist Belief* (Washington, D. C.: Review and Herald Publishing Association, 1957).

"The Spirit of Prophecy" and Ellen G. White

Description. Many religious groups revere a "founder" or a "prophet." SDA leaders admit that some of their earlier writers overstated the dependence of the movement on Mrs. White. The authoritative Adventist position on the relation of Mrs. White's writings and the Bible appears in this quotation from page 93 of *Questions on Doctrine* (hereafter abbreviated *QD*); "While Adventists hold the writings of Ellen G. White in highest esteem, yet these are not the source of our expositions. We base our teachings on the Scriptures, the only foundation of all true Christian doctrine. However, it is our belief that the Holy Spirit opened to her mind important events and called her to give certain instructions for these last days. And inasmuch as these instructions, in our understanding, are in harmony with the Word of God, which Word alone is able to make us wise unto salvation, we as a denomination accept them as inspired counsels from the Lord. But we have never equated them with Scripture as some falsely charge." We read in their official paper, *Review and Herald,* May 14, 1959: "It was with her as it was with the prophets of Old, 'Holy men spake as they were moved by the Holy Spirit' (II Peter 1:21)."

Response. Acquaintance with the SDA movement discloses an inordinately high regard for her writings, even though they are not elevated to the level of the Bible. It is curiously narrow to interpret "the spirit of prophecy" of Revelation 19:10 as a specific reference to this nineteenth-century woman. It is still more puzzling how they can object to the charge that they claim that Mrs. White was inspired, when they themselves say that "it was with her" as it was with the inspired prophets of old.

The Sabbath

Description. Among the "Fundamental Beliefs" of the Seventh-day Adventists is their belief "that the will of God as it relates to moral conduct is comprehended in His law of ten commandments; that these are great moral, unchangeable precepts, binding upon all men, in every age . . . that the fourth commandment of this unchangeable law requires the observance of the seventh-day sabbath" (*QD*, 12). "We believe that the restoration of the Sabbath is indicated in the Bible prophecy of Revelation 14:9-12." (*QD*, 153.) In their current *Know Your Bible Series,* No 27, p. 7, we read: "The Sabbath question is the last great test by which men will decide their eternal destiny."

They believe that just prior to the return of the Lord the issue of observing the seventh-day Sabbath will "become a world-wide test." Those who then refuse to observe the seventh-day Sabbath will receive the mark of the beast mentioned in Revelation 14:11. Those who do observe it (as Adventists do already) constitute the "remnant church." The Seventh-day Adventists take it as their God-appointed task to broadcast the last-day message to all—even Christians of other churches—so they may be privileged to be among the "remnant."

Response. The Christian church as a whole has never continued the Jewish Sabbath. Further research will disclose to any student many quotations taken from the early fathers of the church showing that the transition from the Saturday, seventh-day Sabbath to the Lord's Day—Sunday, the first day of the week—was effected early in the history of the church. Even in the New Testament we find evidences of this shift (John 20:1, 19; Acts 20:7; I Corinthians 16:1, 2).

There is no command in the New Testament to observe the Sabbath. After repeating five of the Ten Commandments, Paul continues, "and if there be any other commandment, it is briefly comprehended in this saying, namely, Thou shalt love thy neighbour as thyself" (Romans 13:9). In the next chapter, he leaves the observance of days neutral: "One man esteemeth one day above another: another esteemeth every day alike. Let every man be fully persuaded in his own mind. He that regardeth the day, regardeth it unto the Lord; and he that regardeth not the day, to the Lord he doth not regard it" (Romans 14:5, 6). This cancels the validity of the SDA insistence of sabbath observance (compare also Colossians 2:16, 17 and Galatians 4:9–11).

The Investigative Judgment

Description. Adventists teach "that the time of the cleansing of the sanctuary . . . is a time of investigative judgment. . . . This investigative judgment determines who of the myriads sleeping in the dust of the earth are worthy of a part in the first resurrection, and who of its living multitudes are worthy of translation" (*QD,* 15). In 1844 Christ moved into the "most holy place" of heaven and took up the work of assessing the conduct of all persons.

Response. John 5:24 says of the believer that he "shall not come into condemnation; but is passed from death unto life." The word here translated *condemnation* is elsewhere translated *judgment.* The same word is used in Romans 8:1: "There is therefore now no *condemnation* to them which are in Christ Jesus." It is here that SDA opens itself to the charge of legalism. "Investigative judgment" is supposed to determine on the basis of conduct who is or is not prepared for eternity. But John 5:24 and Romans 8:1 declare this will not happen to believers. Furthermore, salvation cannot be based upon conduct as investigative judgment requires, for salvation is explicitly "not of works" (Ephesians 2:8, 9). There is, indeed, a judgment of believers yet to come—before the judgment seat of Christ—but that will determine rewards, not admittance to heaven.

Conditional Immortality, "Soul Sleep," and Annihilation

Description. "The condition of man in death is one of unconsciousness." "Immortality is bestowed upon the righteous dead at the second coming of Christ. . ." (*QD,* 13). "The finally impenitent, including Satan, the author of sin, will by the fires of the last day, be reduced to a state of nonexistence" (*QD,* 15). Immortality—the ability to live forever—is not basic to the nature of man. It is a gift of God given to the saved at the time of their resurrection. All who die are merely unconscious. At the last day the wicked will be resurrected only to be totally annihilated by the fires of hell.

Response. The Adventist position overlooks the present tense of eternal life said by the Bible to be the present property of believers. For example, John 3:36 states, "He that believeth on the Son hath everlasting life." How could one have everlasting life if it may be interrupted by death, at which time the person would be unconscious? Paul was willing "to be absent from the body" in order "to be present with the Lord" (II Corinthians 5:8). Immortality, in the light of I Corinthians 15, is achieved at the resurrection. But the wicked too will live endlessly, but in torments (Mark 9:43, 44; Revelation 14:11). The great judgment scene in Matthew 25:31-46 closes with the statement, "And these shall go away into everlasting punishment: but the righteous into life eternal." *Everlasting* and *eternal* translate the same Greek word. We need only to recall the story of the rich man in hell (Luke 16:19-31) to realize the dead are conscious after death.

EVALUATION

1. *The very name "Adventists" calls attention to the return of the Lord.* For this at least we may be thankful. The rise of Adventism was paralleled historically by an increasing interest in prophetic and dispensational studies. While such efforts often give rise to curious

and even erroneous interpretations, there may be the sovereign action of God behind all this in bringing about an increasing emphasis on the imminent return of the Lord.

2. *It is not wise to set dates.* This, it seems, is the persistent peril of prophetic studies. It is not for us to know times. It is for us—as for the first inquisitive disciples—to receive power (Acts 1:6–8). The Lord is coming; that we know. When He shall come, only the Father knows. Since the Great Return is at some definite though unknown time in the future, we are certain that each day moves us twenty-four hours closer to the joy of that hour.

3. *Seventh-day Adventism presents an example of extreme Arminianism.* Arminius asserted the freedom of the will in opposition to John Calvin's predestination teachings. The "investigative judgment" looms before the believer as a goad to good work but it obscures the truth of salvation by faith in the finished work of Christ. One's decisions determine his destiny—a true statement, but one out of balance in Seventh-day Adventism.

4. *Seventh-day Adventism persists in adhering to certain doctrines entirely foreign to historic Christianity.* Among these are the observance of the Sabbath on the seventh day of the week, the investigative judgment, conditional immorality, "soul-sleep," and annihilation of the wicked. Our attitude toward Adventism will continue to be determined in large measure to the significance which we attach to these points of departure from historic Christianity.

5. *There may be true Christians among the Seventh-day Adventists.* God alone is the Judge. If so, they are saved as anyone else—by the blood of Christ. They are Christians not because of their peculiar doctrines, but in spite of them.

FOR FURTHER READING

The latest official source of Seventh-day Adventist doctrine is the huge volume, *Questions on Doctrine.* While large, this volume is simply written and easily understood. It would be the logical starting point for a first-hand study of the movement. That the Adventists do not lack scholarship is obvious from the massive work (four volumes, 3,966 pages) by Leroy E. Froom, *The Prophetic Faith of Our Fathers* (Review and Herald Publishing Association, 1950). This history of prophetic interpretation is widely acclaimed even by non-Adventist scholars.

Published subsequently to *Questions on Doctrine,* and based on it, is Walter R. Martin's book, *The Truth About Seventh-day Adventism* (Zondervan, 1960). As a college student, Dr. Martin observed certain features of the Adventist movement were unfairly treated by evangelicals. After years of thorough research, he produced this most able evangelical response to Seventh-day Adventism. Norman F. Douty, in his more recently published *Another Look at Seventh-day Adventism, With Special References to Questions on Doctrine* (Grand Rapids: Baker Book House 1962), is less conciliatory than is Dr. Martin.

D. M. Canright prefaced his *Seventh-Day Adventism Renounced* (Baker Book House, 1961), with: "Being profoundly convinced that Seventh-day Adventism is a system of error, I feel it necessary to publish what I know of it."

E. B. Jones broke with Adventism after twenty years service, partially as a missionary to India. His pamphlets bear such titles as *Free Indeed, Why You Should Not Be a Seventh-day Adventist, The Answer and the Reasons*. These and other materials are available from the author: address, Guardians of the Faith, P. O. Box B, Traffic Station, Minneapolis 3, Minnesota.

William Biederwolf's pamphlet, *Seventh-Day Adventism* (Eerdman's, n.d.), is somewhat out of date. Louis T. Talbot's *What's Wrong With Seventh-Day Adventism?* (Dunham, n.d.) disagrees with Walter Martin's idea that the Seventh-day Adventists are at root evangelical.

FOR DISCUSSION

1. Describe the origin of Seventh-day Adventism.
2. Why would William Biederwolf call this movement "the result of a predicament"?
3. Explain the "investigative judgment."
4. Why do Christians worship on Sunday?

CHAPTER IV

Out of This World

Spiritualism

"Ye shall know the truth, and the truth shall make you free!" How many cults, how many "founders," have swirled these words as a rallying banner for their cause. Spiritualism is not the only cult that buttresses its spurious gospel with this glowing promise.

Yet these words are not a general statement of fact. They are rather the promised result of a stated condition. "*If* ye continue in my word . . .," said Jesus (John 8:31). There is no truth, no freedom, where there is not the Word of Jesus. Freedom through truth comes by remaining steadfast in Jesus' word. And Jesus' words are found nowhere but in the Bible. Those, therefore, who take a low view of the Bible or of its Lord, by that fact deprive themselves of the condition on which the freeing truth reaches the soul.

Spiritualism, or Spiritism, is one such group. (Either title is used: the group itself uses Spiritualism.)

The "Gospel of Spiritualism" (they use the phrase frequently) is the eerie one of darkened rooms, ghostly appearances, and voices from the spirit world. This gospel will put you in touch with departed "friends." Hence, it understandably flourishes after great wars in which many loved ones died on fields of battle.

The movement has its famous names—most notable Sir Arthur Conan Doyle, creator of the famed character, Sherlock Holmes.

Principally because of its lack of an aggressive missionary policy, its failure to produce a convincing and continuous stream of literature, and its magical elements, the movement has not equalled the growth of other cults. But its inroads are appreciable, especially in South America.

HISTORY

Ancient Spiritualism

Widespread. Death is the most puzzling mystery of life. It is a universal phenomenon, one that has remained unchanged despite all the scientific and cultural development of man. Death is unknown, shrouded in mystery. All men and all nations have sought to interpret it.

The Christian view of death is clear. A man dies, his body is buried, his soul or spirit retains consciousness and is eventually reunited with the body—in a new form, of course—and his interminable existence is then spent either in or out of God's presence. For the Christian, death has lost its sting; for on this earth he already enjoys eternal life.

But those who pondered the problem of death apart from Biblical revelation have often reached the conclusions of Spiritualism. Reports Dr. Van Baalen, "But we do find traces of Spiritism among ancient Chinese, Hindus, Babylonians, and Egyptians; Spiritism can be traced through the Roman Empire and the Europe of medieval times. Of the present-day religious delusions it is therefore the only one which existed in Biblical times, and the Scriptures are anything but silent on it."[1]

Contrasted with Modern Spiritualism. Modern Spiritualism has a specific date of origin and it is now somewhat more than a century old. It appears that modern Spiritualists, similar to Christian Science and Unity, regard the universe as pervaded with a master Spirit whose laws of operation—if known and used—would secure healing and wholeness and would render the category of miracle unnecessary, technically speaking. "Miracles" happen, but they are not interpreted as "interventions in natural law"—as miracles are commonly defined. Instead, they are breakthroughs of a higher form of natural law, whose workings are not yet fully known or are known only to a limited group of "gifted" people—such as mediums or practitioners.

From the *Spiritualist Manual,* official manual of the National Spiritualist Association of Churches, here are the words which demonstrate this contrast between ancient and modern Spiritualism. In the beginning year of 1848, a "spirit intelligence" was disclosed, "an intelligence that was accepted as based on Natural Law and not miraculous or supernatural as heretofore had been accepted. This is the fact that distinguishes Modern from Ancient Spiritualism."[2]

---

[1]Jan Karel Van Baalen, *The Chaos of Cults* (4th ed. rev.; Grand Rapids: Wm. B. Eerdmans Publishing Company, 1962), p. 31.
[2]*Spiritualist Manual* (Milwaukee: National Spiritualist Association of Churches, 1955), p. 74.

Biblical Prohibitions

The Law. The Bible is vividly realistic. It recognizes the reality of spirits in another world—indeed it guarantees life beyond the grave. The neighbors of ancient Israel were beset with sorceries and witchcraft of every sort. When God gave the Law to ancient Israel, He wisely included specific refusals forbidding participation in such black practices.

Here are some specific Biblical references which reveal the Bible's attitude:

1. *Deuteronomy 18:10–12*—"There shall not be found among you any one that maketh his son or his daughter to pass through the fire, or that useth divination, or an observer of times, or an enchanter, or a witch, or a charmer, or a consulter with familiar spirits, or a wizard, or a necromancer. For all that do these things are an abomination unto the Lord: and because of these abominations the Lord thy God doth drive them out from before thee."

2. *Exodus 22:18*—"Thou shalt not suffer a witch to live."

3. *Leviticus 20:6*—"And the soul that turneth after such as have familiar spirits, and after wizards, to go a whoring after them, I will even set my face against that soul, and will cut him off from among his people."

4. *Leviticus 20:27*—"A man also or woman that hath a familiar spirit, or that is a wizard, shall surely be put to death: they shall stone them with stones: their blood shall be upon them."

"Of all the religious source books in the world," summarizes Walter R. Martin, "the Bible unquestionably gives the history of Spiritism in a most concise and dependable form."[3]

Saul and the Witch at Endor. First Samuel 28:7–25 describes the consultation of King Saul with a witch at the town of Endor. However we may explain exactly what happened, note that Saul consulted the witch as a last resort after the Lord refused to answer him "neither by dreams, nor by Urim, nor by prophets" (I Samuel 28:6). Further, Saul himself had cleared the land of such magicians (v. 3). The outcome of Saul's consultation with the witch happened as the Law promised: "So Saul died for his transgression which he committed against the Lord, even against the word of the Lord, which he kept not, and also for asking counsel of one that had a familiar spirit, to enquire of it; and enquired not of the Lord: Therefore he slew him, and turned the kingdom unto David the son of Jesse" (I Chronicles 10:13, 14).

---

[3]Walter R. Martin, *The Rise of the Cults* (Grand Rapids: Zondervan Publishing House, 1955), p. 104.

Modern Spiritualism

Forerunners. Spiritualists themselves are generous in tracing their own ancestry. Persons included would perhaps have been surprised. Emmanuel Swedenborg (1688-1792), for example, began his own cult. But Spiritualists hail his pioneer departures from "orthodoxy."

Andrew Jackson Davis. Called "the John the Baptist of Spiritualism," this uneducated prophet laid the foundation for modern Spiritualism by publishing in 1847 a book entitled *Principles of Nature.* "The full genius and the wonderful mediumship of Andrew Jackson Davis is [*sic*] not yet appreciated by the world. . . . His personal experiences and his extraordinary mediumship truly prepared the way again, for the advent of the ever living Spirit of truth and the reality of spirit manifestation in the Modern World."[4]

The Fox Sisters. March 31, 1848, is the recognized date for the beginning of Modern Spiritualism. On this day, in Hydesville, New York, Margaret and Kate Fox heard "tiny raps" in their father's cottage. The girls were young at the time—some sources say ages six and eight, others eleven and fifteen, still others nine and eleven. These "rappings" were soon discovered to be spelling out a message, so the "Code of Communication" was established thus allegedly opening up intercommunion between this and the spirit world. The girls later admitted these unexplained noises were "childish pranks" produced by "cracking the joints" of their knees. It was this strange and doubtful incident which gave birth to the Spiritualism of today.

Current Status. There are three major bodies of Spiritualists today in the United States, having a total membership exceeding 175,000. This is no true figure of their influence, since the mediums have a sort of private clientele. Morris Pratt Institute in Milwaukee provides a training center. Curiously, the Spiritualists make heavy use of camp meetings. They do not appear to have an extensive literature program, and this factor may account for slower growth than groups like the Mormons and the Jehovah's Witnesses.

DOCTRINES

God as "Infinite Intelligence"

Description. The first item in the "Declaration of Principles" as adopted by the National Spiritualist Association of Churches (perhaps the most representative of Spiritualist groups) reads thus: "We believe in Infinite Intelligence."[5]

---

[4]*Spiritualist Manual*, p. 98.
[5]*Ibid.*, pp. 34, 35.

The attitude of any group toward Christ is of course, crucial. In *The ABC of Spiritualism,* an official Spiritualist document, these indicative questions and answers appear.

15. *Do Spiritualists deny the existence of the historic Jesus?* No. . . . Spiritualists as a body venerate the name and character of Jesus and regard him as the world's greatest Teacher and Exemplar.
16. *Do Spiritualists believe in the divinity of Jesus?* Most assuredly. They believe in the divinity of all men. Every man is divine in that he is a child of God and inherits a spiritual (divine) nature. . . .
17. *Does Spiritualism recognize Jesus as one of the Trinity, co-equal with the Father, and divine in a sense in which divinity is unattainable by other men?* No. Spiritualism accepts him as one of many Saviour Christs, who at different times have come into the world to lighten its darkness and show by precept and example the way of life to men. . . . It recognizes him as a world Saviour but not as 'The only name' given under heaven by which men can be saved. . . .
21. *From the standpoint of Spiritualism how is the character and work of Jesus to be interpreted?* Jesus was a great Mediator, or Medium, who recognized all the fundamental principles of Spiritualism and practiced them.[6]

Response. Such a list of doctrinal ABC's will be viewed as spiralling blasphemy by readers committed to a Biblical view of Christ. This view of God is akin to that of other metaphysical cults and may be described as *pantheism*—the view that all is God and God is all. It is enough to hear Scripture declare, "Neither is there salvation in any other: for there is none other name under heaven given among men, whereby we must be saved" (Acts 4:12).

But these views of God and of Christ will not surprise us if we observe the stated attitude of Spiritualism toward the Bible—always a basic consideration in any doctrinal discussion. The eleventh ABC renders crystal clear how Spiritualists view the Bible:

11. *Is not Spiritualism based upon the Bible?* No. The Bible so far as it is inspired and true is based upon Mediumship and therefore, both Christianity (the simple and beautiful teachings of Jesus—real primitive Christianity) and Spiritualism rest on the same basis. Spiritualism does not depend for its credentials and proofs upon any former revelation."

Clearly then, Spiritualism does not build on the Bible. In this sense it is contrary to the Jehovah's Witnesses, to Unity, to Seventh-day Adventism—all of which claim to be interpreting the Bible. Such a low view of the Bible needs only to be discovered to be condemned.

---

[6]B. F. Austin, *The ABC of Spiritualism* (Milwaukee: National Spiritualist Association of Churches, n.d.).

Communication with the Dead

Description. The distinctive doctrine Spiritualism proclaims is the possibility and benefit of intercommunion between this and the spirit world. "We affirm," reads the fifth item in the "Declaration of Principles," "that communication with the so-called dead is a fact, scientifically proven by the phenomenon of Spiritualism." Messages, so they affirm, come from the spirit world through the agency of a medium—whose function is explained below. Of what value are such "messages"? The eighty-eighth ABC answers: "First to convince men of the continuity of human life. Secondly, to spiritualize our thoughts, affections and lives by instruction and guidance. Thirdly, to bring us consolation in the sorrows and bereavements of life. Fourthly, to enable us to reach through Mediumship exalted and powerful spiritual helpers in the great crises of Life." Yet these "messages" are sometimes trivial and even inaccurate.

Response. Recall the specific prohibitions of the Bible against contacting the unseen world. The Bible does not *deny the possibility* of contacting the spirit world, but it specifically *forbids the practice.* "Witchcraft" is among the works of the flesh listed in Galatians 5:20 as opposed to the fruit of the Spirit. The penalty of attempting to contact the dead, in the Law of Israel, was death. Christians desiring to please God should not take up forbidden practices. Instead they should content themselves with the simple assurances of the gospel that the future and the unseen regions are in the hands of the Creator of things both seen and unseen—a Creator who is also Father to those to whom He gave power to become the sons of God. "But now he is dead," lamented one of the great fathers of the Bible over his dead infant son. "Wherefore should I fast? can I bring him back again? I shall go to him, but he shall not return to me" (II Samuel 12:23).

Salvation by Self-development

Description. On this point, Spiritualism is clear: "From the very nature of the case it may be boldly asserted that no salvation wrought out by any other person can be of any real value to a man. Unless a man takes himself in hand, seeks and follows the truth, and develops the spiritual nature (the Christ) within, no Saviour or system of religion can bring him freedom and peace."[7] From the same book comes the statement, "Every man is divine in that he is

---

[7]*Ibid.,* number 25.

a child of God and inherits a spiritual (divine) nature."[8] The *Spiritualist Manual* includes this paragraph in one of its invocations and readings for worship use: "Believe in self. Know you are a god in embryo! This is the sublimest and most comforting fact in the world, giving assurance of man's individualized eternal existence. . . . Eternal life begins when man begins to live his divinity, the higher side of his character."[9]

Response. The whole idea of vicarious atonement through Christ's shed blood is repugnant to spiritualism. Yet we read in the Word, "Not by works of righteousness which we have done, but according to his mercy he saved us, by the washing of regeneration, and renewing of the Holy Ghost" (Titus 3:5).

No Eternal Punishment

Description. Interpreting its eighth "principle" (which reads, "We affirm that the doorway to reformation is never closed against any human soul here or hereafter"), the *Spiritualist Manual* comments: "We discard entirely the terrible wrong and illogical teachings of eternal damnation and in place thereof we accept and present for consideration of thinking people the thought of the continuity of life beyond the change called death. . . . We accept no such teaching as a 'Hell Fire,' but we do teach that sin and wrong-doing will necessarily bring remorse and suffering that would be difficult to describe in words and which can only be relieved by the individual's own efforts if not here, then in the hereafter."[10]

Response. The following words from the Bible are printed in many editions in red; they are Jesus' own words about the sheep and goat judgment. "And these shall go away into everlasting punishment: But the righteous into life eternal" (Matthew 25:46). This is a statement of Jesus Christ concerning eternal punishment and is the voice of authority to Christians.

Spirit Manifestations

Description. Various avenues are employed by Spiritualists to reach the spirit world. Most common perhaps is the spiritualist medium, a person—man or woman—whom they define as "one whose organism is sensitive to vibrations from the spirit world and through whose instrumentality, intelligences in that world are able to convey messages and produce the phenomena of Spiritualism."[11] Medi-

---

[8]*Ibid.*, number 16.
[9]*The Spiritualist Manual*, p. 64.
[10]*Ibid.*, p. 36.
[11]*Ibid.*, p. 37.

ums conduct seances—meetings in darkened rooms in which eerie manifestations and appearances take place. Raps, unexplainable noises occur and are described as code communications from the spirit world. Voices are heard. Visions are seen. Trances are entered into. The medium actually sleeps during the trance and "lends" his body and vocal cords to the "spirit," who may speak through them. After the seance, the medium may awaken and ask what happened.

Response. Christians know that the devil has strange powers, which are too often underestimated. While Satan is stronger than man, even stronger than the Christian himself, the presence of the Holy Spirit of God within the Christian makes true the promise, "Greater is he that is in you, than he that is in the world" (I John 4:4).

EVALUATION

1. *Spiritualism is antisupernatural.* This seems strange, but it is true. It teaches that all happens according to natural law, and that there is no miracle in the sense of intervention in natural law. For the same reason—belief in unbroken natural law—it denies a personal God.

2. *We do not know everything about the unseen world.* Spiritualism at least demonstrates the reality of the spiritual world, even if it does violate Scriptural principles in pursuit of that world. Scientists today are exploring "ESP"—extra-sensory perception, the apparent existence of realities not capable of measurement by ordinary scientific instruments. Rather than produce gloom, this fact should drive us closer into the bosom of the Father who, in His Word, has told His children all they truly need to know to survive this world and suitably enter the next. Let us let God be God. "The secret things belong unto the Lord our God: but those things which are revealed belong unto us and to our children for ever, that we may do all the words of this law" (Deuteronomy 29:29).

3. *Fraudulent contact with the spirit world is forbidden by the Bible.* The Holy Spirit is more important than the unholy spirits. The Holy Spirit lives within; the spirits dwell without. We are commanded to be filled with the Spirit (Ephesians 5:18) but to avoid seeking "familiar spirits" (Deuteronomy 18:10-12).

4. *Spiritualism clearly and confessedly does not build on the Bible.* This is the fundamental point of cleavage with the evangelical churches. Spiritualism prides itself with being a "progressive religion" and is quite thankful for having been freed from the

fetters of the "Old Theology." This is a very clear example of the most basic issue in theology—what constitutes the accepted source of authority? Accepting the Bible yields a theology whose main outlines appear in all parts of the Christian church and are not blurred by variant interpretations of subsidiary doctrinal points— important as those are. Throwing off Biblical authority, on the other hand, destroys an objective test for doctrine and opens the gate to any number of beliefs that may be spawned by freakish circumstances or fertile imaginations. The Bible is a doctrinal life- guard.

For Further Reading

Exercise caution in using first-hand sources. Two books published by the National Spiritualist Association of Churches, of Milwaukee, have been used here: The *Spiritualist Manual,* (1955 revision), and *The ABC of Spiritualism,* by B. F. Austin. For evangelical criticism, the appropriate sections of the larger books must be consulted. William E. Biederwolf wrote a short pamphlet on *Spiritualism* (Eerdman's, n.d.).

It makes an interesting study to consult Seventh-day Adventist and Jehovah's Witness denials of Spiritualism—since both groups teach anni- hilation and soul-sleep at death.

For Discussion

1. How does the Bible treat Spiritualism?
2. When and where did Modern Spiritualism originate?
3. Is there anything real about spiritualist mediums and seances?
4. What should be the Christian attitude toward Spiritualists and their beliefs?

CHAPTER V

The Mother Church

Christian Science

Most of us go about our business aware that we live and move in an evil world. We who have become Christians have had our own personal share of evil—sin—placed under the atoning blood of Christ. We know, without question, that sin is a very real thing. We can recall when we were gripped by it. And we remember the relief Jesus brought.

But did you know there is a group which teaches that evil does not really exist at all? That sin, death, evil, and pain are only figments of the imagination? That one who believes in the reality of sin and death is enmeshed in "mortal mind" and the scales have not fallen from his eyes yet? That there is really no such thing as sickness? That healing is normal—not miraculous?

There is such a group. They call themselves scientists—Christian Scientists. It is, of course, hard to see how they are either Christian or scientific, having such beliefs as they do.

Nevertheless, there are a million or so who believe this way. Their appeal is largely to the upper classes. Instead of the energetic street-witnessing and doorknocking used by Jehovah's Witnesses, Christian Scientists utilize "Reading Rooms." Like every fast-growing cult, they know the power of the printed page.

It is strange to us to find people calling themselves Christians who redefine all the familiar Christian words we know—atonement, second coming, sin—even the word *God* itself. The Bible treats sin and death as realities. If we hearken to Christian Science, neither of these is real. How much easier it is, and how in line with experience, to accept as true the simple statements of the Bible.

HISTORY

Mary Baker Eddy (1821-1910)

Youth. Like Charles Taze Russell, originator of the Jehovah's Witnesses, Mary Baker Eddy grew up with an orthodox Congregational background. Also like him, she reacted against a strict Calvinistic doctrine of predestination. Here are her own words: "At the age of twelve I was admitted to the Congregational (Trinitarian) Church, my parents having been members of the body for a half-century. . . . The doctrine of unconditional election, or predestination, greatly troubled me; for I was unwilling to be saved, if my brothers and sisters were to be numbered among those who were doomed to perpetual banishment from God. . . . The minister then wished me to tell him when I had experienced a change of heart; but tearfully I had to respond that I could not designate any precise time. Nevertheless he persisted in the assertion that I *had* been truly regenerated, and asked me to say how I felt when the new light dawned within me. . . . He received me into their communion, and my protest with me. My connection with this religious body was retained till I founded a church of my own, built on the basis of Christian Science. . . ."[1]

Mary Baker (*Eddy* was her last married name) appears to have been well-bred. Her writings show a delicate skill in the use of the English language and her whole scheme of religion is highly philosophical. She studied Greek, Hebrew, and Latin from her brother—an outstanding graduate of Dartmouth.

A number and variety of upsetting experiences so affected young Mary that for much of her life she was disturbed emotionally and physically. Her father had said, "Her brain is too big for her body," and insisted that she be forbidden to study so much. Her condition of health led her to experiments with various types of healing vying for attention in the last century—such as spiritualism, water therapy, and hypnotism. It accounts also in part for the whole emphasis of Christian Science on healing of mind and body.

Three Marriages. Some of these crises she experienced were marital. At age twenty-two, she married a businessman, George W. Glover, who loved her deeply. But he died of fever a few months before the arrival of their first child. Her second marriage, at thirty-two, was to an amorous dentist, Dr. Daniel Patterson. "I was compelled," writes Mrs. Eddy, "to ask for a bill of divorce, which was granted me in the city of Salem, Massachusetts." Her third marriage took place in 1877 when Mrs. Eddy was fifty-six years old. Asa Gilbert Eddy, "the first student publicly to announce himself a Christian Scientist," became her husband and her helper.

It is curious to hear Mrs. Eddy write off these very human exper-

---

[1] Mary Baker Eddy, *Retrospection and Introspection* (Boston: Published by the Trustees Under the Will of Mary Baker Eddy, 1920), pp. 13–15.

iences as unreal. But the belief that only mind is real characterizes her religion and prompts this digression in her autobiography: "It is well to know, dear reader, that our material, mortal history is but the record of dreams, not of man's real existence, and the dream has no place in the Science of being. . . . Mere historic incidents and personal events are frivolous and of no moment, unless they illustrate the ethics of Truth."[2]

Discovery of "Science." The year 1866, at age forty-five, is the date Mrs. Eddy gives for her great discovery that became the basis of Christian Science. This was a mental discovery, a conclusion reached over a period of years. Two paragraphs from her autobiography tell us about it—and about her: "Thus it was when the moment arrived of the heart's bridal to more spiritual existence. When the door opened, I was waiting and watching; and, lo, the bridegroom came! The character of Christ was illuminated by the midnight torches of Spirit. My heart knew its Redeemer. He whom my affections had diligently sought was as the One 'altogether lovely,' as 'the chiefest,' the only, 'among ten thousand.' Soulless famine had fled. Agnosticism, pantheism, and theosophy were void. Being beautiful, its substance, cause, and currents were God and his idea. I had touched the hem of Christian Science. . . .

"I named it *Christian*, because it is compassionate, helpful, and spiritual. God I called *immortal Mind*. That which sins, suffers, and dies, I named *mortal mind*. The physical senses, of sensuous nature, I called *error* and *shadow*. Soul I denominated *substance*, because Soul alone is truly substantial. God I characterized as individual entity, but His corporeality I denied. The real I claimed as eternal; and its antipodes, or the temporal, I described as unreal. Spirit I called the *reality*; and matter, the *unreality*."[3]

Science and Health. In 1875, Mrs. Eddy's "discovery" was shared with the world in the publication of the chief source book of Christian Science called in full *Science and Health, with Key to the Scriptures.* The book was variously greeted, with reactions ranging from considering it nonsense to treating it as revelation. The book contains thirteen chapters treating subjects like Prayer, Atonement, Physiology, Creation, and more difficult ones like Science, Theology, Medicine, and one on the Science of Being. The final summarizing chapter is followed by the second part of the work, the "Key to the Scriptures"—which is little more than a spiritualizing explanation of Genesis and of Revelation.

---

[2]*Ibid.*, p. 21.
[3]*Ibid.*, pp. 23, 25.

Plagiarism. When material produced by one author is used by a second author without credit to the first, the second author is guilty of plagiarism. Mrs. Eddy herself experienced other writers misusing her materials, and she has severe words against plagiarism. However, she stands charged with plagiarism herself. A certain scholar named Francis Lieber had produced a manuscript on the philosophy of the German Philosopher Hegel. After a thorough review of the facts of the case, Walter R. Martin reports: "It is demonstrably true that Mrs. Eddy copied thirty-three pages verbatim and one hundred pages in substance into *Science and Health, with Key to the Scriptures,* edition 1875, from Dr. Lieber's manuscript on the writings of Hegel, a manuscript antedating *Science and Health* and now in the possession of the Princeton Theological Seminary in Princeton, New Jersey."[4]

Phineas Parkhurst Quimby

"Doctor." Mrs. Eddy studied under and was treated by "Dr." Quimby, a self-styled healer whose popularity peaked about this time. From 1862-1864 she was his student.

The Quimby Manuscripts. While Mrs. Eddy and her followers deny vehemently any such thing, the evidence points to the conviction that, as Dr. Martin concludes, "To Phineas Parkhurst Quimby, *not* Mary Baker Eddy, goes the dubious honor of being the 'discoverer' of the principles upon which Mrs. Eddy built her entire philosophical superstructure."[5]

Growth.

Organization. In 1879 a charter was obtained and the Church of Christ, Scientist, was formally initiated. Two years later the Massachusetts Metaphysical College was opened to train future Scientists. In 1894 a massive, quarter-million dollar structure became The First Church of Christ, Scientist—the "Mother Church" for all Scientists.

Current Status. Church rules forbid the counting of members, but an estimated million persons are taken up with the teachings of Mary Baker Eddy. Christian Science Reading Rooms are found in every town of size, and a variety of publications reinforce the ideas of the founder. The church has a special appeal to the wealthy.

---

[4]Walter R. Martin, *Christian Science* (Grand Rapids: Zondervan Publishing House, 1957), p. 7. See also chapters I to IV in the full-length book by the same author, *The Christian Science Myth* (Zondervan Publishing House, 1955).

[5]Martin, *The Christian Science Myth,* p. 54.

DOCTRINES

The teachings and writings of Mary Baker Eddy are somewhat difficult to understand, being highly philosophical. The vocabulary itself is extensive, and this difficulty is compounded by the double sense attached to words by Scientists. In outlining the teachings, we shall concentrate on defining them. Their criticism will be immediately obvious to those familiar with Scripture.

Spiritualizing the Scriptures

Description. One of the basic features of Christian Science is its refusal to accept the ordinary meaning of Biblical language. One of their editors summarized a sermon by Mrs. Eddy with these words, in part: "She affirmed that the Scriptures cannot properly be interpreted in a literal way. The truths they teach must be spiritually discerned, before their message can be borne fully to our minds and hearts. . . . The literal rendering of the Scriptures makes them nothing valuable, but often is the foundation of unbelief and hopelessness. The metaphysical rendering is health and peace and hope for all. The literal or material reading is reading of the carnal mind, which is enmity toward God, Spirit."[6]

Response. If the simple, obvious meaning of Scripture is tossed away, doctrinal chaos can easily follow. Understanding this to be their starting point, one will not be surprised to find many of the basic teachings of Christianity reinterpreted by Christian Scientists. It is necessary when interpreting the Scripture to assume that the language means what it says, unless some other portion of the Bible indicates that the passage is to be interpreted figuratively.

God Is Not a Person

Description. The Glossary in *Science and Health* gives the following definition: "GOD: The great I AM; the all-knowing, all-seeing, all-acting, all-wise, all-loving, and eternal; Principle; Mind; Soul; Spirit; Life; Truth; Love; all substance; intelligence." Mrs. Eddy's writing entitled *No and Yes* answers the question, "Is there a personal deity?" with the following words, in part: "God is Love; and Love is Principle, not person. . . . When the term divine Principle is used to signify Deity it may seem distant or cold, until better apprehended. This Principle is Mind, substance, Life, Truth, Love. When understood, Principle is found to be the only term that fully

---

[6]Mary Baker Eddy, *Miscellaneous Writings* (Boston: The Christian Science Publishing Society, 1896), p. 169.

conveys the ideas of God—one Mind, a perfect man, and divine Science."[7]

The Biblical understanding of the Trinity, as might be expected, is not accepted by Christian Scientists. Their attitude toward Christ appears in a later section. And who or what is the Holy Spirit? "In the words of St. John: 'He shall give you another Comforter, that he may abide with you *forever*.' This Comforter I [Mary Baker Eddy speaking] understand to be Divine Science.' "[8]

Response. Identifying the Holy Spirit with "Divine Science" is a variety of blasphemy. We must agree that God is love (I John 4:8), but we also know that God performs the act of loving (John 3:16). Christian Science confuses the *nature* of God with one of His *attributes.*

Jesus Did Not Die

Description. In fact, no one dies. Death is not real. "His disciples believed Jesus to be dead while he was hidden in the sepulchre, whereas he was alive, demonstrating within the narrow tomb the power of Spirit to overrule mortal, material sense."[9] With no true death, there could have been no true payment for sin. So Christian Scientists do not see the atonement as a vicarious sacrifice. "It was not to appease the wrath of God, but to show the allness of Love and the nothingness of hate, sin, and death, that Jesus Suffered."[10] "The second appearing of Jesus is, unquestionably, the spiritual advent of the advancing idea of God, as in Christian Science."[11] And here is the sum: "Jesus of Nazareth was a natural and divine Scientist. He. . .was a Christian Scientist."[12]

Response. When Christian Science denies the death of Christ, it makes Christ a liar. Jesus plainly told His disciples He was going to die (Mark 8:31; Luke 9:22). Further, Paul stated in Romans 5:8, "Christ died for us," and in I Corinthians 15:3, "Christ died for our sins." The Bible must be taken for what it says.

Identification of Jesus as "a Christian Scientist" recalls the Spiritualist claim that He is "a medium." Such exclusivistic (and mutually contradictory) claims exemplify a common cult character-

[7]Mary Baker Eddy, *No and Yes* (Boston: Published by the Trustees Under the Will of Mary Baker Eddy, 1924), pp. 19, 20.

[8]Mary Baker Eddy, *Science and Health, with Key to the Scriptures* (Boston: Published by the Trustees Under the Will of Mary Baker Eddy, 1934), p. 55.

[9]*Ibid.*, p. 44.

[10]Eddy, *No and Yes*, p. 35.

[11]Eddy, *Retrospection and Introspection*, p. 70.

[12]*Ibid.*, p. 26.

istic—adoption of a restricted view of God. This is what J. B. Phillips calls belief in a "God-in-a-Box."

Sin, Death, and Evil Are Unreal

Description. "Hence there is no sin, for God's Kingdom is everywhere and supreme, and it follows that the human kingdom is nowhere, and must be unreal."[13] Explains *Science and Health*: "Error is a supposition that pleasure and pain, that intelligence, substance, life are existent in matter. . . . Therefore the only reality of sin, sickness, or death is the awful fact that unrealities seem real to human, erring, belief until God strips off their disguise. They are not true, because they are not of God."[14]

Response. Tucked away in Proverbs 16:4 is a verse worth noticing: "The *Lord* hath made all things for himself: yea, even the wicked for the day of evil." The Bible does not deny the existence of evil, but it asserts that God is greater than evil and that He will finally triumph.

The lingering belief in evil's reality Christian Scientists explain by saying this belief is due to "mortal mind." The only evil there is, then, is that imagined by "mortal mind." Dr. Gerstner's criticism is devastating: "But mortal mind itself is never explained away. . . . If it is said to be unreal then all other evil comes alive again. Mortal mind is the nemisis of the cult's theology: Christian Science cannot explain it or explain it away; it cannot affirm it or deny it; it cannot live with it or without it. Mortal mind is mortal to Christian Science—the Frankenstein which destroys its creator."[15]

EVALUATION

1. *Christian Science is totally unbiblical.* Its opposition to the Scriptures does not appear in the form of denial. Mrs. Eddy quotes the Bible regularly—if erringly. But the assumption that evil is unreal and the idea that some sort of mystical sense must be obtained before Scripture can be interpreted—these notions cross the simplicity of the Scriptures. There is more to lining up with Biblical truth than merely asserting the truth of the Scriptures. There is such a thing as a view of life that is diffused throughout the entire Bible. Such a view Christian Science does not share.

2. *The gospel of Christian Science is largely philosophical.* It presents one answer to the great problem of evil: how could a

---

[13]*Ibid.*, p. 35.
[14]Eddy, *Science and Health*, p. 472.
[15]Harold Lindsell, *et al.*, *The Challenge of the Cults* (Grand Rapids: Zondervan Publishing House, 1961), p. 17.

loving God permit suffering? Christian Science answers: He does not. They get rid of evil by saying it does not exist. We find this hard to believe. But we can understand why some highly intellectual persons deeply disturbed over the existence of evil, and not accepting the simple assurances of the gospel, find some comfort in just flatly denying evil exists. At least, that is one way out—if not a very convincing one.

3. *Can Christian Science heal?* This is a different question from asking, "Do healings take place within Christian Science?" Here we must be cautious. If the Christian Scientists will produce testimony after testimony showing Christian Science did heal, recognized scholars like Walter R. Martin will produce testimony after testimony showing Christian Science did not heal. We may believe both reports to some extent at least. Edward Kimball writes in a widely distributed Christian Science pamphlet, ". . .a physician of understanding, if he will be candid, will say that seventy-five or eighty per cent of all the cases of sickness that occur would recover spontaneously if they were left alone."[16] Does this statistic not apply as well to Christian Science?

Further, recent studies show conclusively some illnesses begin with ideas. If the ideas can be corrected the disease will vanish. This concept is known as psychosomatic medicine. It may be then, that there are some recoveries for some sicknesses under Christian Science. If so, they take place not because of Christian Science, but in spite of it.

Christian Scientists, incidentally, do not interpret healing as miraculous. They reject miracles. Healing, they say, is merely the outworking of God's law.

And if there be a thoroughly proved instance of an incurable organic disease healed under the auspices of Christian Science, let us reread Matthew 7:22, 23: "Many will say to me in that day, Lord, Lord, have we not prophesied in thy name? and in thy name have cast out devils? and in thy name done many wonderful works? And then will I profess unto them, I never knew you: depart from me, ye that work iniquity."

For Further Reading

Christian Science Reading Rooms usually operate a free lending library. If you wish to check original sources while following a more thorough exposition of Christian Science, obtain a copy of *Science and*

---

[16]Edward A. Kimball, *Answers to Questions Concerning Christian Science* (Boston: The Christian Science Publishing Society, 1937), p. 27.

Health, with Key to the Scriptures. Mary Baker Eddy's other works have been compressed into a single volume titled *Prose Works.* One of the writings it contains in *Retrospection and Introspection*—her autobiography in less than a hundred pages. Page number references may not always work out, since there are many editions of the various works.

In most any bus or train station or in any airport one may discover free sample copies of the *Christian Science Sentinel* (weekly) or the *Christian Science Journal* (monthly). The *Christian Science Monitor* is one of the country's most highly respected newspapers. It limits its religious propaganda to a single item daily which is also translated into German and French.

A major volume of evangelical criticism on Christian Science was written by Walter R. Martin and Norman H. Klann. It is entitled *The Christian Science Myth* (Zondervan, 1955), and it presents a thorough exposé of the plagiarism, origin, and teachings of the group. Walter Martin himself has written a smaller pamphlet of very practical use, *Christian Science* (Zondervan, 1957).

Louis Talbot has one of his series about cults entitled, *What's Wrong with Christian Science?* George W. Wittmer discusses not only the defective doctrines, but also the life of Mary Baker Eddy and the organizational structure of the church. His 58-page pamphlet is entitled *Christian Science in the Light of the Bible* (Concordia, 1958).

FOR DISCUSSION

1. Did Mary Baker Eddy have a happy childhood?
2. How does Christian Science describe God? Where do you differ?
3. How does Christian Science account for the existence of evil? How do you?
4. How do you explain the physical healings claimed by Christian Science practitioners?

CHAPTER VI

Armageddon Ahead

Jehovah's Witnesses

Have you ever been asked to buy a copy of *Awake!* or *The Watchtower?* If you did not have the required nickel, chances are that middle-aged lady or aggressive gentleman would offer you a free copy, perhaps paying for it themselves. For they are dedicated to their task. They are Jehovah's Witnesses.

By standing on the busy street corner and selling the magazines from their little white bags, they are—they think—fulfilling Christ's prophecy recorded in Matthew 24:14, "And this gospel of the kingdom shall be preached in all the world for a witness unto all nations; and then shall the end come." There are thousands of other "publishers" like them sowing the "Witness" word in more than one hundred fifty countries around the world.

Though Jehovah's Witnesses officially adopted that title in 1931, they are often referred to by other names—Watch Tower Bible and Tract Society, People's Pulpit Association, International Bible Students Association. "Russellites" fits better a splinter group—the Dawn Bible Students.

Part of the appeal of the Jehovah's Witnesses is the high regard they appear to have for the Bible and Bible study. But no group truly based on the teachings of the Bible could deny—as do the Witnesses—the deity of Christ, whom they call "God's Chief Son."

As with most cult groups, the Bible is interpreted through certain outside writings. As in Seventh-day Adventism, the Witnesses deny the immortality of the soul and assert the annihilation of the wicked. Like Mormonism, Seventh-day Adventism, Spiritualism, and Unity, the Jehovah's Witnesses have an American origin.

HISTORY

Jehovah's Witnesses have been led in turn by a "Pastor," a "Judge," and a "President." Here is a brief view of each, together with the dates of their leadership.

"Pastor" Russell: 1870–1916

Haberdasher. Near Pittsburgh, Pennsylvania, in February of 1852, a son was born to parents of Scotch-Irish Presbyterian descent. His name was Charles Taze Russell. Reared in Allegheny—an old name for Pittsburgh's North Side—he became at twenty-five a successful businessman selling men's goods.

Organizer. His business ability carried over into his church activities. Congregational in background, Russell early rejected the severe Calvinistic doctrine that eternal torments awaited all but the elect. By fifteen he was a skeptic. But he was soon led to restudy the Bible for himself. Without adequate preparation, he worked out a scheme of understanding the Bible to which this day rests as the theological foundation of the Jehovah's Witnesses. In 1870 he organized a Bible study group in Pittsburgh and six years later was appointed its "pastor," though he was never ordained as the word is commonly used.

In 1879 he financed and founded *Zion's Watch Tower*—a periodical which soared in circulation from 6000 in that year to an astounding 3.8 million in 1961. Ten years later he began Zion's Watch Tower Tract Society, later renamed The Watch Tower Bible and Tract Society. This and similar societies print an enormous quantity of literature which is widely spread by "publishers" found in hundreds of cities, all over the world. Jehovah's Witnesses owe their existence to this man.

Defendant. The life and morals of "Pastor" Russell have always been questionable to say the least. Over the issue of alleged improper relations with another woman and over policy differences in administering Zion's activities, Mrs. Russell separated from her husband in 1897. Six years later a divorce suit was brought and a separation awarded in 1906. Still later the "Pastor" had to pay $6,036 in back alimony, payment of which he had avoided by a bogus transfer of holdings.

Plaintiff. Much of the history of the Jehovah's Witnesses is written on court records. The life of their founder is no exception, and certainly it set the pattern. In the first decade of the present century, the "Pastor" offered for sale—at one dollar per pound—some "Miracle Wheat" promised to outgrow other seeds five times. A newspaper labeled the claims a fake, and Russell brought suit for $100,000. Russell lost when government examiners could find no distinctive superiority in the grain. Before another court in Canada, Russell was forced to admit he could not read Greek—which he had sworn under oath he could. This made him guilty of perjury.

Writer. The new doctrines of the "Pastor" were widely broadcast by the forceful personality and literary talents of their originator. His major work came in six volumes entitled *Studies in the Scriptures.* If a choice had to be made, he claimed, it would be better to read his books than the Bible.[1] All told about sixteen million copies of his writings have been distributed in thirty-five languages.

Returning from one of his many lecture tours, Charles Taze Russell died aboard a train in Texas on October 16, 1916.

"Judge" Rutherford: 1916-1942

Lawyer. A few months after Russell's death, Joseph F. Rutherford assumed his predecessor's mantle. Preaching Russell's funeral, he gave the founder a special privilege. Unlike other men—who according to Jehovah's Witnesses' teaching are simply unconscious at death—Russell stood now in God's presence. A practicing lawyer in Missouri, "Judge" Rutherford became intrigued with the "Pastor's" teachings. The two met in a Kansas City hotel. Russell suggested Rutherford write about God's plan "from the lawyer's point of view." Rutherford did. And, henceforth, he dedicated his talents to the growing movement.

Leader. Immediately upon appointment the "Judge" threw his vast array of abilities into guiding the group Russell had founded. Fearing no one, he seemed to thrive on court cases. Persecution for the Russellites was common. It strengthened them. Rutherford lashed out against "organized religion," by which he meant Christianity in general. With a stroke, he wrote off the whole history of the church as apostate. Ministers with honorary D.D. degrees (for "Doctor of Divinity") were labeled *"dumb dogs."* The attacks were sustained and vicious.

Writer. "Judge" Rutherford wrote even more than "Pastor" Russell. He produced a hundred books which were distributed in eighty languages. In appearances he was imposing. Tall, aggressive, fluent, he held a sort of personal magnetism which greatly augmented his leadership.

Schismatic. In the late twenties a group who favored Russell's teachings—some of which Rutherford had repudiated— broke off to form the Dawn Bible Students. There are about 25,000 members. They sponsor the "Frank and Ernest" radio broadcast and circulate *The Dawn* magazine.

---

[1]The full quotation, taken from p. 298 of the September 15, 1910, issue of *The Watchtower,* is cited by Walter R. Martin in *Jehovah of the Watchtower* (3rd ed. rev.; Grand Rapids: Zondervan Publishing House, 1956), p. 24.

"President" Knorr: 1942 to Present

Growth. Taking over when Rutherford died in 1942, Nathan H. Knorr has since guided the Witnesses. This has been a period of tremendous growth. Their "Kingdom Halls" fill the land. By 1950 the Jehovah's Witnesses had been billed as "America's fastest growing religion."

Statistics. The 1962 *Yearbook for American Churches* cites a letter to its editor from the Society in which 4,170 congregations with 250,000 members are listed for the United States. World-wide membership is 916,332. There are no figures for ministers, since Jehovah's Witnesses consider every member a minister. Therefore they have as many members as ministers, a viewpoint Christians would do well to consider.

Much of the success of the Jehovah's Witnesses is due to their massive literary efforts. They offer 350-page, hardbound books for fifty cents. Their "New World Translation" of the New Testament, a volume altered to support their denial of Christ's deity, sells for a single dollar. Two magazines of thirty-two pages each cost a mere five cents. *The Watchtower* in 1961 was distributed in 60 languages and 3,800,000 copies. *Awake!* had a circulation of 3,250,000 in 23 languages. This literature comes from a huge plant in Brooklyn where dedicated workers are paid, in addition to room and board, fourteen dollars a month.

They operate radio station WBBR at 1330 kilocycles, with a power of 5000 watts, in Brooklyn. At South Lansing, New York, is "Gilead"—an unaccredited, short-term Bible school which in its first dozen years of operation (beginning 1943) sent out nearly eighteen hundred missionaries.

Between 1942 and 1952 the Jehovah's Witnesses' North American membership doubled. It is easy to understand why this group poses a serious challenge to the Christian church.

DOCTRINES

What message do the Witnesses offer that accounts for their successes? Essentially it is a message that appeals to the hopes of man. It is a message of a New World about to come.

One of the Witnesses' five-cent pamphlets is entitled *"This Good News of the Kingdom."* It is a compact survey of their message. We shall quote from it extensively to discover their beliefs in their own words. (Unless noted otherwise, page numbers refer to this booklet.)

Jehovah the Only God: Christ His "Chief Son"

Description. Jehovah's Witnesses vehemently deny the Trinity. The Holy Spirit is but the power of God—not personal, not divine. "There is only one true God who is almighty and supreme. . . . Everyone who wants life, including his chief Son, Christ Jesus, must recognize His supremacy and be subject to him" (p. 5). "Jesus and Jehovah God are not the same person, nor is Jesus equal to God. Jehovah alone is supreme" (p. 6).

Response. The Biblical teaching of the Trinity arises from the fact that there are three Personages recognized as divine—Father, Son, and Spirit. See the abundant evidence in Genesis 1:26; Matthew 28:19; I Corinthians 12:4–6; I Peter 1:2; I John 5:7, 8.

Denial of the deity of Jesus Christ. His essential equality with God the Father, removes the Witnesses from the borders of Christianity. "For in him dwelleth all the fulness of the Godhead bodily" (Colossians 2:9). "In the beginning was the Word, and the Word was with God, and the Word was God" (John 1:1). "For he, who had always been God by nature, did not cling to his prerogatives as God's equal, but stripped himself of all privilege by consenting to be a slave by nature and being born as mortal man" (Philippians 2:6, 7, Phillips Translation).

Ransom Atonement

Description. Recognizing that man is a sinner—though their conception of sin is not deep—Jehovah's Witnesses describe redemption as a ransom. "Thus Jehovah God by sending his Son Jesus Christ to earth provided through him and his death a ransom price. . . . By means of the ransom Christ Jesus bought back this that was lost, namely, perfect human life with its rights and earthly prospects" (p. 13). It is precisely the human life of Jesus that was the ransom price. Having forfeited this human life, He could not take it up again and He was, therefore, resurrected a "spirit creature." "The Bible shows that by means of the ransom some would be granted life in the heavens, others on the earth" (p. 15).

Response. Notice that what was lost and, therefore, needed to be redeemed was not spiritual life but "perfect human life with its rights and earthly prospects"—*earthly* prospects. According to this cult, Jesus' death merely restored man's right to live an untroubled life of perfection on earth. There is little consciousness here of sin as a high offense against a holy God and the need for a vicarious atonement by Christ, through His blood, so both God's righteousness and holiness could be satisfied. In Matthew 20:28 and Mark 10:45 the death of Jesus is described as a ransom, but John 1:29 and I Peter 2:24 show that the object was release from sin, not merely the securing of earthly bliss. Jehovah's Witnesses have an inadequate understanding of sin, salvation, redemption, and vicarious atonement by blood.

"Millions Now Living Will Never Die"

Description. This title is often advertised as an address to be given. Their idea is that within the present generation God will by "King Jesus" shortly destroy the forces of Satan at the Battle of Armageddon. When this happens, Satan will be totally annihilated forever, and those who have accepted the messages of the Witness "publishers" will live happily ever after on a remade earth.

Response. One evangelical minister devised a neat counter to the Jehovah's Witnesses when they advertised a lecture of the above title. Based on Ephesians 2:1, he announced his sermon subject as, "Millions Now Living Are Already Dead." This earth-bound hope of the Witnesses shows their religion to be devoid of the hope of heaven and marks their appeal to fleshly desires for ease without repentance.

Second Coming Took Place in 1914

Description. "When Jesus said he would come again he did not mean he would return in the flesh visible to men on earth. He has given up that earthly life as a ransom and therefore cannot take such life back again. . . . The good news today is that Christ Jesus has come again, that God's kingdom by him has been set up and is now ruling in heaven. . ." (p. 19). "All the evidence shows that Jesus took up his Kingdom power and began his reign from heaven in the year 1914" (p. 21).

What proof do they offer that Christ "returned" in 1914? They point to Matthew 24:3, 7, 8, where wars, famines, earthquakes, and sorrows are foretold as signs of the Lord's Return. "In the years 1914 to 1918 thirty nations were engaged in war with one another, and it was therefore called the First World War. . . . Also, since 1914 there have been reported more earthquakes than ever before in history. . . . Today there is fear of yet another war using more terrible weapons of destruction" (pp. 20, 21).

Response. True enough, these are promised signs of the Lord's return. What the Jehovah's Witnesses overlook is that that return was promised to be visible: "Ye men of Galilee, why stand ye gazing up into heaven? this same Jesus, which is taken up from you into heaven, shall so come in like manner as ye have seen him go into heaven" (Acts 1:11). The same chapter to which the Witnesses point for the signs also contains the promise, ". . .and then shall all the tribes of the earth mourn, and they shall see the Son of man coming in the clouds of heaven with power and great glory" (Matthew 24:30). A single verse refutes their notion of a "spirit resurrection" of Christ, one in which He, therefore, had no body. After His resurrection, Jesus said to those who also doubted His physical resurrection, "Behold my hands and my feet, that it is I myself: handle me, and see; for a spirit hath not flesh and bones, as ye see me have" (Luke 24:39).

No Endless Hell

Description. "Some religious organizations hold out the prospect of either life in heaven or eternal torment in a hell-fire. As we have seen, the Bible does not support the idea of eternal torment and it does not limit the hope of future life in peace and happiness only to heaven" (p. 18). "So then, when a person dies his soul does not go straight to heaven, nor does his soul go to a place of torment called 'hell' " (p.11). "The simple truth about the matter is that when a person dies, he is dead, unconscious, and knows nothing" (p. 12).

Response. Jehovah's Witnesses share with Seventh-day Adventists the belief in soul sleep—that people cease to exist when they die. The two groups likewise share the belief that the destiny of the wicked is total annihilation. The soul, these groups teach, is never separated from the body. If the body dies, so does the soul. That this idea is erroneous is clear from Matthew 10:28: "And fear not them which kill the body, but are not able to kill the soul: but rather fear him which is able to destroy both soul and body in hell" (see also Revelation 20:15).

Unpatriotic Practices

Description. For a long time, Jehovah's Witnesses have stood steadfast in their refusal to salute the American flag—or any other for that matter. "Hence no witness of Jehovah, who ascribes salvation only to Him, may salute any national emblem without violating Jehovah's commandment against idolatry as stated in his

Word."[2] Beginning about 1945, they reached the conclusion, announced through *The Watchtower,* that blood transfusions were contrary to the law of God. This they derived from an obvious misunderstanding of Leviticus 17:10–14. They refuse to bear arms and stand opposed to military service of any type—even noncombatant.

Response. These teachings need only be recited to demonstrate their error. It is indeed ironic that the Witnesses refuse to salute and serve the country that, by its insistence on freedom of religion, has repeatedly favored this minority group by court decisions guaranteeing their liberty.

EVALUATION

1. *Jehovah's Witnesses present a coarse, earth-bound gospel.* They have no hope of the visible return of Christ or of everlasting joy in the presence of God in heaven. "Jehovah's Witnesses are social gospelers and have invented a social gospel which completely overshadows that of the Modernists."[3] This is an attempt to reach the "new world" without the personal regeneration demanded by the gospel of the new birth.

2. *Works are prominent here as among all cults.* "In order to gain Jehovah's final approval," explains *"This Good News of the Kingdom,"* one must "remain faithful to Jehovah right on down to Armageddon and on into the new world. If you want to be one of these persons, then you must prove yourself to be the kind of person that Jehovah would want in his new world" (p. 30). The Christian conception of grace—the unmerited favor of a loving God—thus disappears.

3. *Their reliance on the Bible accounts in part for the success of the Jehovah's Witnesses.* They recognize the Bible as the sole Word of God, unique in its inspiration. Today, if asked, they will disclaim placing the writings of Russell or Rutherford on the same level. It happens that most people believe in the Bible even though they are ignorant of its teachings. This is a disastrous condition, one easily taken advantage of by any Witness schooled in a few stock "Greek" and "Hebrew" explanations which greatly impress the untrained common man. Here is a forceful plea for thorough Bible study and teaching in church and at home.

4. *Christians can learn a lesson from the Witnesses about the*

[2]*"Let God Be True"* (2nd ed. rev.; Brooklyn: Watchtower Bible and Tract Society, Inc., 1952), p. 243.
[3]F. E. Mayer, *Jehovah's Witnesses* (St. Louis Concordia Publishing House, 1957), p. 45.

power of the printed Word. No account of the success of the Jehovah's Witnesses can omit the major part played by the printing press, accompanied by willing and persistent "publishers" who thrust the literature into every corner of the world. The Christian church has not yet seen the power of the tract. Literature for the lost will bring light or blight—depending on its content.

FOR FURTHER READING

The magazines *Awake!* and *The Watchtower* are easily available first-hand sources. The reader may be surprised to discover some material here that is of general interest—not merely Jehovah's Witnesses propaganda. *Let God Be True* is a readable and official doctrinal summary—over 300 pages. The writings of Russell and Rutherford are too numerous to mention and may be found in the books listed below. A non-member, Marley Cole, wrote a sympathetic and somewhat varnished account in *Jehovah's Witnesses* (Vantage, 1955).

Walter R. Martin collaborated with Norman H. Klann to produce an exposé of the movement, *Jehovah of the Watchtower* (Zondervan, 1956). A recent, thorough doctrinal analysis from an evangelical viewpoint may be found in *The Theology of Jehovah's Witnesses* (Zondervan, 1962), written by George D. McKinney, Jr. For a book that may be given directly to a Witness, William J. Schnell's *Thirty Years a Watch Tower Slave* (Baker, 1956) is most satisfactory. The writer himself left the Witnesses after a generation of service. He has also published a discussion of their doctrines in his second work, *Into the Light of Christianity* (Baker, 1959).

Several pamphlets may be mentioned: Louis Talbot, *What's Wrong With Jehovah's Witnesses?* (Dunham, n.d.); William E. Biederwolf's *Russellism Unveiled* (Eerdmans, n.d.); Herbert Lockyer *Jehovah's Witnesses Exposed* (Zondervan, 1959); and F. E. Mayer, *Jehovah's Witnesses* (Concordia, 1957). The last of these has a most thorough doctrinal analysis.

For a factual survey of the history and doctrine of the Jehovah's Witnesses, together with a list of Scripture references countering their errors, see the appropriate chapter in Walter R. Martin's book, *The Rise of the Cults* (Zondervan, 1955).

FOR DISCUSSION

1. When did the Jehovah's Winesses group begin? Name their three leaders.
2. According to their teaching, when, how, and why did Christ come?
3. Explain their statement, "Millions now living will never die."
4. What do you think accounts for their phenomenal growth?

CHAPTER VII

"Earth Has No Sorrow"

Unity

"Earth has no sorrow that heaven cannot heal"—a good motto, and a Biblical one. But one also conditioned on full acceptance of, and obedience to, all the words of Jesus—particularly His "hard sayings" demanding confession of personal inward sin and whole-hearted repentance. Many cults, even more individuals, seek the benefits of the gospel while suppressing its demands.

The Unity School of Christianity of Lee's Summit, Missouri, offers prosperity and health to all people of all faiths. They have no membership. You do not have to leave your former denomination to associate with them. They do not insist that their teachings be regarded as infallible. But they do offer peace and prosperity to all.

Charles Fillmore, himself a wealthy realtor, believed in *Prosperity*. His book bearing that title preserves his rendition of the favorite Twenty-third Psalm. Here are a few lines:

> The Lord is my banker; my credit is good. He maketh me to lie down in the consciousness of omnipotent abundance; He giveth me the key to His strongbox. He restoreth my faith in His riches, He guideth me in the paths of prosperity for His name's sake. Yea, though I walk through the very shadow of debt, I shall fear no evil, for Thou art with me; Thy silver and gold, they secure me. . . .[1]

"We have in Unity," writes Charles W. Ferguson "an enormous mail-order concern dispensing health and happiness on the large scale of modern business enterprise. . . . It suggests pretty well what Americans want in the realm of the spirit."[2]

---

[1]Quoted by Jan Karl Van Baalen, *The Chaos of Cults* (4th ed. rev.; Grand Rapids: Wm. B. Eerdmans Publishing Company, 1962), pp. 137, 138.

[2]Charles W. Ferguson, *The Confusion of Tongues* (Garden City, New York: Doran and Company, 1929), p. 230.

HISTORY

Sources

Mesmerism. The origins of Unity and the other mind-healing cults go back to the experimentation of an Austrian physician named Franz Anton Mesmer (1734-1815). Forerunner of Sigmund Freud, Mesmer early investigated imagined relationships between the celestial bodies and human sicknesses. Though his views were never scientifically accepted, his influence opened the door of research on the interrelationships between mind and body which today constitutes the field of psychotherapy. "Mesmerism" is but another name for hypnotism, and the work of its founder paved the way for the mind-healing cults.

Transcendentalism. A belief forming the background of Unity, Transcendentalism was a movement in nineteenth-century American literature—most notably associated with the name and writings of Ralph Waldo Emerson (1803-1882). Writers holding this philosophy of life stressed realities beyond the world of sense. The mind-healing cults habitually disparage the sense world.

Christian Science. The Unity group is sometimes traced to the religion of Mary Baker Eddy. The founders of Unity were greatly influenced by persons who had been associated with Mary Baker Eddy. A Unity periodical for a while bore the name *Christian Science Thought.* But the Unity School does not wish to be understood as an offshoot of Christian Science. It rather traces its origin to the same common interests in new methods of theological interpretation which, in another line of development, yielded Christian Science. "Our views," wrote the founder in an early periodical, "are not those of orthodox Christian Science."[3] One of the major differences between Unity and Christian Science is the variant description of evil. While Christian Science denies that evil exists in any real sense of the term, Unity admits that evil exists but pays little attention to it.

Charles and Myrtle Fillmore

The Realtor. Young Charles Fillmore grew up near St. Cloud, Minnesota, during days when trade with Indians was common. A skating accident when he was twelve left him with a shortened leg from which—in all his ninety-four years—he never fully recovered. As a lad in St. Cloud, he was attracted to the writings of

---

[3]Quoted by James Dillet Freeman, *The Story of Unity* (Lee's Summit, Missouri: Unity School of Christianity, 1954), p. 58.

James Russell Lowell and Ralph Waldo Emerson through the influence of a companion's mother, an educated army officer's wife. He worked at various jobs—printer's apprentice, grocery and bank clerk, railroad clerk, mule team driver. Traveling in the West, he finally assembled a sizeable fortune in a real estate boom in Pueblo, Colorado.

Like Joseph Smith, the Mormon prophet, Charles Fillmore purposed to go straight to God for truth—so diverse were the opinions of various religions. He did, however, dabble in Buddhism, Brahmanism, Theosophy, Rosicrucianism—even Christianity. He had experimented with Spiritualism and had been in seances with a medium. This religious acquaintance, with his fascination for Lowell and Emerson, foreshadowed the multiple sources of present-day Unity.

Leaving Colorado, Fillmore came to Kansas City and engaged in extensive real estate development. The present headquarters of Unity—Lee's Summit, Missouri—lies to the south of Kansas City.

The Methodist. Charles Fillmore's companion in the founding of Unity was his wife—Myrtle Page, nine years his senior. They met at a literary club in Denison, Texas, where Charles had gone to work and Myrtle to teach. Myrtle was reared in Pagetown, Ohio, the daughter of respected citizens active in the local Methodist Episcopal church. Myrtle herself "had been brought up in the belief that she was an invalid and had inherited a tendency to tuberculosis."[4] One wonders if this is the Unity way of saying she was an invalid.

The Great Discovery. After suffering for some time Myrtle Fillmore, accompanied by her husband, attended a lecture in Kansas City in the spring of 1886. The speaker was a Dr. E. B. Weeks, who had come from the Illinois Metaphysical College founded shortly before by Emma Curtis Hopkins. Emma Hopkins served under Mary Baker Eddy as an editor of the *Christian Science Journal.* But she left Mrs. Eddy over some doctrinal disagreements. It was at this lecture Myrtle Fillmore discovered a promising fact. Here is how Unity tells the story: "Charles Fillmore came away from that lecture long ago feeling no different than when he had gone, but the woman who walked out of the hall on his arm was not the same woman who had entered it. A new, a different, a liberating, a transforming conviction was blazing in her

---

[4]*Ibid.*, p. 30.

heart and mind. . . . As she walked from the hall, one statement repeated itself over and over in her mind: 'I am a child of God and therefore I do not inherit sickness.' "[5]

By this discovery, the claim is, she eventually received healing. Sharing her testimony, she began receiving calls from others to help them in their conditions.

The Covenant. Myrtle Fillmore's "discovery" occurred in 1886. Her husband at this time was involved in his real-estate business. But he became interested, and the two of them spent some time in Chicago studying under Emma Curtis Hopkins, the erstwhile *Christian Science* editor and now director of a metaphysical college. By 1889 they founded a magazine, first called *Modern Truth*. Changed later to *Christian Science Truth*, the title varied until 1891. In that year Charles Fillmore heard a voice; it said, "Unity!" " 'That's it!' he cried out. 'Unity!' he told the others. 'Unity! that's the name for our work, the name we've been looking for.' "[6]

The next year the two Fillmores signed a covenant. Discovered only in 1942 in Charles' own handwriting, it breathes the optimistic cheerfulness of the Unity School:

> **Dedication and Covenant**
>
> We, Charles Fillmore and Myrtle Fillmore, husband and wife, hereby dedicate ourselves, our time, our money, all we have and all we expect to have, to the Spirit of Truth, and through it, to the Society of Silent Unity.
>
> It being understood and agreed that the said spirit of Truth shall render unto us an equivalent for this dedication, in peace of mind, health of body, wisdom, understanding, love, life and an abundant supply of all things necessary to meet every want without our making any of these things the object of our existence.
>
> In the presence of the Conscious Mind of Christ Jesus, this 7th day of December, A.D. 1892.
>
> Charles Fillmore
> Myrtle Fillmore[7]

Thus was launched the great ship Unity School of Christianity.

Growth and Organization

The Fillmore Sons. Two sons of Charles and Myrtle Fillmore are largely responsible for the mushrooming growth of Unity.

---

[5]*Ibid.*, p. 44.
[6]*Ibid.*, pp. 61, 62.
[7]A photographic reproduction of this "covenant" may be found on the inside front cover of the pamphlet *Unity School of Christianity* (Lee's Summit, Missouri: Unity School of Christianity, n.d.).

Lowell Fillmore, born in 1882, is the organizing force behind Unity headquarters. He is the current president of the group. His brother Rickert has been the builder and architect of the vast Unity Village south of Kansas City.

Lee's Summit, Missouri. Over a beautiful area, covering over 1200 acres, Unity Village spreads gracefully and beautifully. Here over 700 persons help produce and distribute 60,000,000 pieces of printed literature each year. Five hundred weekly broadcasts fan out from 120 stations. A correspondence school gives lessons in "Truth." A completely equipped training school offers a variety of courses to anyone seriously interested—regardless of religious faith or affiliation. At the Village, precisely at 11 a.m. daily, all machinery stops and all workers stop for silent prayer. The voice of Charles Fillmore reciting the Lord's Prayer is broadcast by recording throughout the grounds. One of the most widely publicized aspects of Unity is the "Silent Unity." A group of 140 workers "pray" for any and all requests sent in by letter, wire, or telephone call. Some 600,000 such calls are handled yearly. A Unity Inn and Unity Motel are operated for the many visitors and students. They advertise the best vegetarian cafeteria in the world, though they do not insist on a vegetarian diet.

Since they consider themselves a "school of practical Christianity," and do not require severing any previous denomination connections, there are no membership figures to report. There are, however, about 265 "Unity Centers" (mostly in the United States), which parallel local churches. "My guess," reports Marcus Bach, noted scholar of religious groups, "is that more than one-third of denominationally identified Christians in the United States have read or are reading Unity material. One reporter stated that nine-tenths of all Unity literature goes into Protestant homes."[8]

DOCTRINES

The varied background of Charles Fillmore has already been described. Unity reflects this selective method of doctrinal formulation. "It was 30 years," writes James D. Freeman of founder Charles Fillmore, "before students induced him to write out a statement of faith." This he qualified with the words: "We are hereby giving warning that we shall not be bound to this tentative statement of what Unity believes. We may change our mind to-

---

[8]"Pioneer in 'Positive Thinking,'" *Christian Century*, March 20, 1957, p. 357.

morrow on some of the points, and if we do, we shall feel free to make a new statement."[9]

Another Unity writer notes with pride: "Unity has no dogmatic statement of faith to which each student is required to subscribe, nor does it ask its followers to agree with every proposition it makes. Rather it invites a person to accept what he finds helpful in his efforts to lift his consciousness above the level of the ordinary and somewhat destructive view of life."[10]

Thus in its very attitude toward doctrine, Unity rejects a strictly Biblical orthodoxy. The Scriptures recognize a certain set of beliefs as crucial and vital, and not open to individual option. There is a "faith" which was "once delivered unto the saints" for which we should "contend" (Jude 3). There is a gospel which makes any "other gospel" accursed (Galatians 1:6–9). So even before we look at specific Unity teachings, we must criticize sharply their reluctance toward doctrinal finality.

The Bible Not Infallible

Description. "We believe that the Word of God is the thought of God expressed in creative ideas and that these ideas are the primal attributes of all enduring entities in the universe, visible and invisible. The Logos of the first chapter of the Gospel of John is the God idea or Christ that produced Jesus, the perfect man. We believe that the Scriptures are the testimonials of men who have in a measure apprehended the divine Logos but that their writings should not be taken as final."[11] "Unity School believes that the Bible's greatest value may not be found in a study of its literal meaning. We see that its writings have another meaning."[12] "Unity seeks to interpret the Bible. All its teachings are based on it. . . . Unity does not claim that its interpretation of Biblical statements is infallible or that it is final. It holds that as man's spiritual consciousness expands he will receive ever-increasing revelations of Truth."[13]

Response. It is enough for those who accept the authority of the Bible to be reminded of two passages of Scripture: II Timothy

---

[9]James Dillet Freeman, *What is Unity?* (Lee's Summit, Missouri: Unity School of Christianity, n.d.), p. 5.

[10]Elizabeth Sand Turner, *What Unity Teaches* (Lee's Summit, Missouri: Unity School of Christianity, n.d.), p. 3.

[11]*Unity's Statement of Faith* (Lee's Summit, Missouri: Unity School of Christianity, n.d.), part 27.

[12]*Unity School of Christianity*, p. 14.

[13]Turner, *op. cit.*, p. 5.

3:16: "All Scripture is given by inspiration of God. . . ." II Peter 1:20, 21: "Knowing this first, that no prophecy of the Scripture is of any private interpretation. For the prophecy came not in old time by the will of man: but holy men of God spake as they were moved by the Holy Ghost."

God Is Principle

Description. "We believe in God, the one and only omnipotent, omniscient, and omnipresent Spirit-mind. . . . We believe that creative Mind, God, is masculine and feminine, and that these attributes of Being are fundamental in both natural and spiritual man. . . . We believe that we live, move and have our being in God-Mind; also that God-Mind lives, moves, and has being in us, to the extent of our consciousness. . . . Almighty Father-Mother, we thank Thee for this vision of Thine omnipotence, omniscience, and omnipresence in us and in all that we think and do, in the name of Jesus Christ, Amen!"[14] "Unity believes that God is spirit. . . . Spirit is the life principle, the breath of the Almighty, animating all forms of life and the universe itself."[15]

Response. This teaching makes of God an abstract principle rather than a living person. Designating God as "Father-Mother" and addressing prayer to such a principle reveals the presence of truth within error—always the subtly attractive thing about error. There is, in the Biblical view of the world, a sharp distinction between man and his Creator and again between these and the created world. Unity approaches a view known as pantheism—the notion everything is soaked in God, and that God is everywhere and is everything. Opposing this, the great revelation about God given by Jesus pictures God as a loving, personal Father—not an impersonal Father-Mother principle. Recall the vivid portrayal of the loving Father in the parable of the Prodigal Son, which G. Campbell Morgan has renamed "the parable of the Father's heart" (Luke 16:19–31).

Jesus and "the Inner Christ"

Description. According to Unity, there is an "inner Christ" resident within all men. Jesus is Christ because He above all men expressed perfectly this "inner Christ." "The difference between Him and us is not one of inherent spiritual capacity but a difference in demonstration of it. Jesus was potentially perfect and He

---

[14]*Unity's Statement of Faith*, parts 1, 16, 17, 30.
[15]Turner, *op. cit.*, pp. 5, 6.

expressed that perfection; we are potentially perfect, but we have not expressed it. . . . Jesus attained a divine awareness and un-foldment without parallel in this period of the world's history."[16]

Response. Such a view lowers Christ and elevates man. It makes of Jesus "the perfect man." But hear the Bible: "Looking for that blessed hope, and the glorious appearing of the great God and our Saviour Jesus Christ" (Titus 2:13). "For there is not a just man upon earth, that doeth good, and sinneth not" (Ecclesiastes 7:20). "But of him are ye in Christ Jesus, who of God is made unto us . . . righteousness. . ." (I Corinthians 1:30).

Salvation by Attainment and by At-one-ment

Description. "We believe that through conscious union with Jesus in the regeneration man can transform his body and make it perpetually healthy, therefore immortal, and that he can attain eternal life in this way and in no other way."[17] Unity believes in positive prayer by affirmation, rather than by supplication. "Strong statements of Truth, in the form of affirmation and denial, become the lever by which man lifts himself out of the pit that he has dug for himself."[18]

Response. Breaking the word *atonement* into at-one-ment fully describes Christ's vicarious atonement if we understand the at-one-ment to be a union with God in which the identity neither of God nor of man is lost and if such state be conceived as substitu-tionary redemption from damning sin. But Unity uses this word to mean a mystical absorption into the God-Spirit-Principle of the universe. Redemption is ever "not by works of righteousness which we have done" (Titus 3:5). Regeneration is spiritual rebirth, not merely sliding from "sense consciousness," into "spiritual con-sciousness."

Reincarnation

Description. "We believe that the dissolution of spirit, soul, and body, caused by death is annulled by rebirth of the same spirit and soul in another body here on earth. We believe the repeated incarnations of man to be a merciful provision of our loving Father to the end that all may have opportunity to attain im-mortality through regeneration as did Jesus."[19]

Response. This lingering belief in Unity, which as with other

---

[16]*Ibid.,* pp. 8, 9.
[17]*Unity's Statement of Faith,* part 19.
[18]*Unity School of Christianity,* p. 10.
[19]*Unity's Statement of Faith,* part 22.

beliefs they allow may or may not be accepted, is doubtless a carry-over from Charles Fillmore's explorations in the Eastern religions. Quite simply, the Bible says ". . . it is appointed unto men once to die, but after this the judgment" (Hebrews 9:27).

EVALUATION

1. *There is some specific value in "positive thinking."* Philippians 4:8 provides Biblical advice to think positively. Marcus Bach calls Unity the "pioneer in positive thinking." This emphasis has been picked up by others in the church world today, notably Norman Vincent Peale. It has also appeared in some Pentecostal circles emphasizing prosperity. Built on top of a vital regenerated Christian experience, positive thinking is good advice. But the peril is that it is often offered, as in Unity, apart from the gospel demands for confession and repentance of recognized sin.

2. *As with the Jehovah's Witnesses, Unity is concerned with the here and now.* It is a gospel of the present, not of the future. Reincarnation brings one back again into this present world. Such emphasis tends to obscure Christian certainties of the future.

3. *Unity does not sense the reality of sin and evil.* They teach that these exist but that they are not enduring. Christian Science denies the existence of evil: Unity ignores the *presence* of evil. The Bible treats sin as very real, but assures us of Christ's victory over it.

4. *There is more to Christianity than prosperity.* Someone has noted that the promise of the Old Testament is blessing in *prosperity,* while the promise of the New Testament is blessing in *adversity.* The prosperity that counts is that of the soul (III John 3). A Homeless Carpenter once wisely said, "A man's life consisteth not in the abundance of the things which he possesseth" (Luke 12:15)

FOR FURTHER READING

The Story of Unity, by James Dillet Freeman, presents their own history in popular form. Pamphlets useful for first-hand study include *Unity's Statement of Faith, What Unity Teaches, Unity School of Christianity,* and *What is Unity?*—a reprint of one part of the *Christian Herald* series. These may all be obtained from the Unity School of Christianity, Lee's Summit, Missouri.

Ample evangelical criticism may be found in Walter R. Martin's pamphlet *Unity,* in which he promises a forthcoming major volume to be entitled "The Unity Cult Unmasked." One answer to the question *What's Wrong with Unity School of Christianity?* (Dunham, n.d.) is summarized by Louis T. Talbot.

A wide variety of Unity periodicals, ranging from *Wee Wisdom* to *Good Business,* clearly reveals Unity's doctrinal flexibility.

FOR DISCUSSION

1. Recall the various sources of Unity.
2. What was Myrtle Fillmore's "great discovery"?
3. Is there such a thing as "fixed doctrine"?
4. How legitimate are "positive thinking" and "prosperity"?

CHAPTER VIII

World-Changing

Moral Re-Armament

Many of the sects and cults trace their origin to one man—or quite possibly to one woman. Mormons honor Joseph Smith, Seventh-day Adventists build on Ellen G. White, Christian Science traces to Mary Baker Eddy, Spiritualism goes back to the Fox Sisters, Unity to Charles and Myrtle Fillmore. Others are similar. Even recognized Christian churches have revered founders: Martin Luther and the Lutherans, John Wesley and the Methodists, for two conspicuous examples.

The movement studied in this lesson builds on the life and experience of one man, a lifelong bachelor, Frank N. D. Buchman. Reporting his recent death, *Time* magazine described him this way: "An improbable prophet, ovoid and owlish, with a piping voice and a slangy sweetness-and-light that in the past four decades won him an earnest following."[1]

While others reached the down-and-outers, Frank Buchman sought the upper level of society; he performed "soul surgery" on the "up-and-outers." Moral Re-Armament has a high-level appeal. It gained its biggest thrust—indeed it acquired an earlier name from the relationship—through its association with Oxford University in England.

Like the Unity School of Christianity, it cuts across denominational barriers. Anyone can belong to "MRA," as it is commonly abbreviated. There is no membership, save that of active application of its principles and association with its activities.

Its workers labor without pay, reminding one of the Jehovah's Witnesses who labor in Brooklyn for their keep plus a meager monthly allowance. Or of the Mormon youth who dedicate two years of their lives without pay.

Equipped with an idea, MRA undertakes to change the world

---

[1]August 18, 1961, p. 59.

by changing individuals. But the change sought does not quite reach Christian conversion.

HISTORY

Various Names

Oxford Group. The study of the names of the major cults and of their derivation would make an interesting and informative pursuit. As many of the other cults, MRA has other names. Best known, and probably earliest, is "the Oxford Group." This name was scribbled on the pullman car compartment of a South African train in 1928 by a porter who had heard only that "a group from Oxford" University was occupying that particular compartment. The name stuck. Frank Buchman, as we see below, had singular success in "soul surgery" at Oxford University among cultured collegians. Sometimes the group is called "the Oxford Movement" or "the New Groupers." An individual member may be referred to as a "grouper."

Moral Re-Armament. On Frank Buchman's sixtieth birthday, he renamed his movement "Moral Re-Armament." The world at the time (1938) was in the throes of World War II, and there was much talk abroad about "re-armament." It occurred to Frank Buchman that what was needed was *moral* re-armament. So he gave that name to a movement whose aim it clearly expressed.

Other Names. Little used today is the title *Buchmanism,* or *Buchmanites.* The likewise infrequent caption, "The First Century Christian Fellowship," discloses their interest in personal relationships.

Frank N. D. Buchman (1878-1961)

Early Training. Frank Buchman was born in 1878—three years after Mary Baker Eddy published *Science and Health,* and the very year "Pastor" Russell started printing the magazine later to become *The Watchtower.* He was born in Pennsburg, Pennsylvania and was reared a Lutheran.

Graduating from the Lutheran schools, Muhlenburg College and Mount Airy Seminary, he was ordained a Lutheran minister in 1902. Lutheran clergymen vow to uphold Scripture, and Frank Buchman never renounced his vow.

When a seminary companion accused him of professional ambition, Frank Buchman took up the unpromising and impoverished pastorate in Overbrook, near Philadelphia. Here, he began a boys' settlement house, but he then resigned over disputes with six board members. Dismayed, he toured Italy, then went to England.

Keswick Experience. The town of Keswick, England, is a synonym for "deeper life" in that land. Annual Bible conferences bring outstanding Christian leaders who explore before concerned Christians the oportunities and obligations of deep commitment.

But it was not to a great Bible conference that Frank Buchman went. It was to a small church where seventeen people were listening to a lady preacher. Frank Buchman's own later description of what happened at this meeting bears all the earmarks of a genuine cataclysmic spiritual experiment: "The woman's simple truth personalized the Cross for me that day and suddenly I had a poignant vision of the Crucified. There was infinite suffering on the face of the Master and I realized for the first time the great abyss separating myself from Him. That was all, but it produced in me a vibrant feeling as though a strong current of life had suddenly been poured into me and afterwards a dazed sense of great spiritual shaking up. There was no longer the feeling of a divided will, no sense of calculation or argument, or oppression and helplessness; a wave of strong emotion following the will to surrender rose up within me from the depths of an estranged spiritual life and seemed to lift my soul from its anchorage of selfishness, bearing it across that great sundering abyss to the foot of the Cross."[2]

From this account, it appears that Frank Buchman had an evangelical beginning at least. Indeed, this movement has always preserved a core of Christian truth and its doctrinal unconcern relieves it from setting up any specifically anti-Christian teachings.

This experience left Buchman with a definition of true Christian experience as involving primarily the will, rather than the intellect or the emotions. That definition introduces a voluntary aspect of "life changing" which, if overstressed, squeezes out of conversion the necessary saving function of God.

Spread of "Buchmanism." In 1909 Frank Buchman became Secretary of the Y.M.C.A. at Pennsylvania State College, thus continuing his work with young men and stimulating the characteristic individual approach. Abroad a decade later, Buchman in 1921 formed the "Oxford Group" by inviting serious undergraduates to one of his "house parties." The movement spread rapidly: Holland in 1927, South Africa in 1928, Canada from 1932-1934.

---

[2]Quoted by Charles Braden, *These Also Believe,* p. 404.

Denmark in 1935, and Sweden in 1938. Now, the movement is world-wide.

House Parties. A distinctive technique successfully developed by Frank Buchman and since widely used by MRA is the house party. The first of these took place in China in 1918. One hundred guests met at the house of a well-to-do lawyer. Such gatherings make for informality and allow more extensive and friendly contact than would be possible in a church service. At these parties games are played and refreshments are served, but the feature is personal testimonies of persons whose lives had changed. Often, confessions are recited publicly as a prelude to deeper spiritual advance.

All this sounds orthodox enough. And it is. The church today could make aggressive use of the old-fashioned virtue of hospitality often relinquished in the name of a false breed of "separation" and "holiness." Can there be anything wrong about inviting unconverted acquaintances into the influence of a Christian home?

Buchman's practice took him to the homes of the wealthy who could afford lavish house parties. It explains somewhat the appeal of the group to higher levels and it teaches the wisdom of adapting method to mission.

Caution is needed in controlling confession in such meetings. There is no virtue, and there is potential harm, in parading past sins in detail. Some of Buchman's house parties gained an unsavory reputation because of overemphasis on confession of fleshly sins. This technique, however, is doubtless one factor in the success of the movement.

Current Status

World Headquarters. Costing nearly a quarter-million dollars, Moral Re-Armament in 1946 set up international headquarters in neutralist Switzerland. Purchased from the Swiss government, the property consists of two former hotels and several chalets overlooking Lake Geneva and the French Alps. From here, international efforts—now tied in with politics and economics of the Western world—are directed. A First World Assembly convened in 1947 with delegates from around the world. Elaborate, multimillion dollar quarters also stand ready for a thousand guests on Mackinac Island, Michigan.

International Acceptance. The current mission of Moral Re-Armament appears to be international peacemaking. The message is, "To change the world, we must change individuals." It insists on moral reform. In the shadow of possible self-destruction, concerned leaders of the world so recently thrust into the space age welcome Buchman's emphasis on personal morality. A few quotations from significant people will illustrate:

> *Chancellor Konrad Adenauer of West Germany*: "Moral Re-Armament has played an invisible, but effective part in bridging differences of opinion between negotiating parties in important international agreements."

> *Prime Minister Kishi of Japan*: "But for Moral Re-Armament Japan would be under Communist control today. Our greatest need now is to go on the offensive and make Moral Re-Armament the policy of our government and our people."

> *President Kasavubu of Kenya*: "You have found the secret of liberation for Africa. All men must think how to give this moral basis to the country."[3]

MRA then finds wide acceptance among world-wide governmental leaders because of its emphasis upon personal morality in an age when the continued existence of the human race depends upon the uncertain maintenance of certain ethical standards. Whether MRA has a sufficient basis for the morality it seeks is the issue which focuses doubt on its evangelical adequacy.

Films and Plays. We have noted that MRA appeals predominantly to the upper levels of society. There is another method, in addition to the house party, successfully employed in reaching this segment. An advocate of MRA writes, "Plays and films have been powerful weapons in taking the ideology of Moral Re-Armament to the world. The effort to reach the millions by films has now been greatly accelerated by the building of a T.V.–film studio on Mackinac Island."[4]

PRACTICES

Some of the specific devices employed by MRA we have already observed—the house party, films, plays, interdenominational action. But there are several groups of virtues and practices which have been heralded as slogans by the group. These we may examine after noting a reprehensible doctrinal unconcern.

Lack of Doctrinal Commitment

Description. MRA has no creed. It draws *sponsors* rather than *members*. It is interested in moral action rather than theological belief. "The chief difficulty," writes Horton Davies, "in attempting to set forth its teaching is that this organization seems to remain

---

[3]*The Discerner*, Vol. III April–June, 1961, number 10, p. 12.
[4]George A. West, "Moral Re-Armament," *Christian Herald*, July, 1961, p. 59.

interdenominational at the cost of freeing itself from any positive doctrinal commitments. It may, therefore, better be considered as a system, a way of life, rather than as a creed."[5] And another authority notes, "There are no theological statements on such vital Christian truths as the person and work of Christ."[6]

Response. Being a follower of Christ requires believing the words He spoke. There is an essential list of beliefs, a minimum list but an essential list, which must be "those things which are most surely believed among us" (Luke 1:1). MRA discounts acceptance of theological statements as necessary, though it does not at all object to anyone's beliefs. Remember that Frank Buchman became convinced that true religion is not what you *feel* or what you *believe* but what you *do*. Right living is necessary, but only belief in Christ can produce right living.

The Five C's

At least three groups of words put into memorable slogans the things regarded as important by MRA. The first, the earliest, of these was "the five C's." These are: Conviction, Contrition, Confession, Conversion, and Continuance.

This series represents the sequence through which one goes in bringing about a "life change." It does no harm to recognize the truth in this series. The fundamental criticism of MRA is not error but inadequacy.

The Four Absolutes

One whose life has been changed should now point toward key virtues called "the four absolutes." In every phase of living, the MRA devotee strives for: absolute honesty, absolute purity, absolute unselfishness, and absolute love.

These goals are worthy enough. But we should recall they approximate the "fruit of the Spirit" itemized in Galatians 5:22, 23.

The Four Principles

How are these virtues to be obtained? There are four ways: sharing, surrender, restitution, and guidance.

A major point is made in taking steps to secure restitution of past shortcomings. When Frank Buchman experienced spiritual

---

[5]Horton Davies, *The Challenge of the Sects* (Philadelphia: The Westminster Press, 1961), pp. 139ff.
[6]F. E. Mayer, *The Religious Bodies of America* (4th ed. rev.; St. Louis: Concordia Publishing House, 1961), p. 498.

renewal in England he sat down immediately and wrote to the six board members against whom he had lodged ill will. The letter read like this:

> My Dear Friend,
>   I have nursed ill-will against you. I am sorry.
> Forgive me?
>
>   Yours sincerely,
>   Frank

Though unacknowledged, the letters were effective in repairing relations with the board members.

On guidance, Frank Buchman also has specific ideas. He describes prayer as "listening," and suggests "listening" with pad and pencil in hand to record any impressions given. MRA has a saying: "When man listens, God speaks. When man obeys, God acts. When God acts, nations change."[7]

EVALUATION

1. *There is much Christians can learn from Moral Re-Armament.* It does no harm to be rearmed morally. The house party opens an evangelistic avenue whose potential has not been tapped. Christians may do well to invite uncommitted companions into their homes for special meals. Prayer and preparation can guide the conversation into the sphere of spiritual realities. Or, even the example of a Christian home—without spoken words—has a convincing eloquence all its own. Use has already been made of Christian films, an instrument employed by MRA.

The techniques for spiritual advance likewise reveal worth. MRA urges restitution—too often a conveniently forgotten obligation. Confession one to another was James' advice before it ever occurred to Frank Buchman (James 5:16). There is, as Buchman taught, a "listening" aspect to prayer. But of course the Bible makes room for supplication also. And who would question the legitimacy of the "four absolutes"—honesty, purity, unselfishness, and love? The demand for surrender is a constant concern to many Christians, and sharing is but a good translation for the New Testament word *fellowship*.

2. *The fundamental defect of Moral Re-Armament is not its error, but its inadequacy.* Nor what MRA says, but what it does not say creates dissatisfaction for many. It is too silent about the deep-rooted character of sin. It centers in man's need rather than in God's provision—both of which should be held in balance.

---

[7]Quoted by Davies, *op. cit.*, p. 142.

It neglects factors of divine spiritual dealings direct with the individual as a necessary prelude to human acts of the will which secure a "life change."

3. *Moral Re-Armament overemphasizes personal experience.* Some evangelical groups do the opposite in stressing intellectual apprehension at the expense of personal appropriation. The desirable balance personally posesses the mentally understood truth. Personal experience without theological foundation leads to a fanciful mysticism. Theological foundation without personal experience leads to frigid orthodoxy. By personally accepting Christ as Saviour and heeding the words He spoke, which are recorded only in the Bible, it is possible to avoid the dangerous dimension in either direction.

4. *Doctrine is important.* A statement of beliefs is crucial for any person or group. We must have some solid framework of accepted facts on which to ground faith and action. It is because of a lack of sufficient appreciation for—and understanding of— basic Christian doctrines that the cults flourish today. MRA can have its international success cutting through many major denominations only because it offends no doctrinal creeds. "The Hindu, Muslim, the Buddhist, as well as the Protestant, the Catholic, and the Jew find they can unite on this basis of a moral theology."[8] But Christian morality stems from Christ, and the doctrine of Christ is sometimes exclusive and offensive to other beliefs.

5. *Moral Re-Armament addresses itself to the critical international political situation.* It stands as a foe to Communism, urging personal then national moral reformation as the only certain cure. Placing the international headquarters in peace-loving Switzerland is certainly symbolical and not likely accidental. Christians should address themselves to the situation in which the world stands this crucial hour. But the message thus proclaimed should be that ancient one of the claims of Christ.

6. *Moral Re-Armament, unlike most of the other cults. is not laden with specific teachings contrary to Biblical perspective.* Its weakness lies in its inadequate doctrinal basis. Its strength lies in its personal approach, including insistence upon "life change" —even though this change more nearly approaches reformation than regeneration. Horton Davies' estimate of the movement is worth quoting: "M.R.A. may be regarded as a foe of the Christian church in its lack of interest in doctrine; but its supporters are

---

[8]West, *op. cit.*, p. 60.

more significantly identified as the gadflies of the Church than as its heretics. The Church has the light: it needs the warmth of Moral Re-armament."[9]

For Further Reading

In consulting books on cults, be certain to recall the different names of the group. Look for Moral Re-Armament, the Oxford Group, or Buchmanism.

Any public library can supply the January 9, 1956 issue of *Time* magazine. On pages 76 and 77 you will find a double-page spread consisting of an illustrated paid advertisement featuring "an idea to save the world."

Dr. Van Baalen cites as additional significant books on Moral Re-Armament *Inside Buchmanism* (Philosophical Library, 1954), by Geoffrey Williamson, and *For Sinners Only* (Harper, 1932), by A. J. Russell.

For Discussion

1. Do you think Frank Buchman's Keswick experience was a genuine Christian conversion?
2. What techniques of communication has MRA adapted to its ends?
3. What limitations would you suggest for public confession?
4. Why is doctrine important?
5. In what ways does Moral Re-Armament differ from other cults?
6. What would be the best way to rearm morally?

---

[9]Davies, *op. cit.*, p. 149.

CHAPTER IX

Out of the East

Oriental Cults

Geography divides the world into the Orient and the Occident. Lands east of the Mediterranean constitute the Orient. Those west of that region make up the Occident.

The major religions originated in the Orient. Christianity itself began in Palestine—an Oriental land. So did Judaism, out of which Christianity flowered. Mohammedanism, third great world religion, likewise began in the same vicinity.

Other significant world religions are prominent in the East. Hinduism, Taoism, Confucianism, Shintoism, Sikhism, Parsiism—all are found far to the east of the Great Sea.

Several important American cults may be traced either directly or indirectly to this part of the world. The Unity School of Christianity, already examined, teaches reincarnation—a typical and persistent Eastern doctrine. In this chapter we shall review the impact of several cults which are dominantly oriental in nature. The theology of these groups tends to be exceedingly complex and baffling, requiring intensive study or even some "special revelation" (as they claim) to comprehend.

Eastern religious thought tends to be mysterious and mystical. Someone has noted that the Oriental saint has his eyes *shut,* while the Christian saint has his eyes *open.* Much is made in the Orient of silent meditation. There also we find an impersonal God, rather than the personal Father Jesus talked about. Even this impersonal God the cultists often confuse with the universe itself, mistaking one for the other.

As you observe the origin and beliefs of these Oriental cults, note by contrast the simplicity of the gospel and its universal availability.

THEOSOPHY

History

Ancient Origins. The word *theosophy* means literally "the wisdom of God." The movement called by that name may be traced back into history for hundreds, even thousands, of years. Several of its most prominent teachings derive from ancient Hinduism whose earliest origins reach back to 3000 B.C.

Helena Petrovna Blavatsky (1831-1891). Modern Theosophy begins with the life and influence of a Russian-born woman of accomplishment. Helena Petrovna was born in 1831 in the town of Eksterinsoslav, Russia, just a year after Joseph Smith organized the Mormon church. At the age of seventeen or eighteen, and apparently to spite her governess, Helena married a General Blavatsky, who was then forty-eight years old. The marriage lasted three months.

From 1848 to 1873, "H.P.B.," as she is known, traveled extensively throughout the world. She became interested in the newly revived Spiritualism. For a time, she was a medium—a fact of no small importance in evaluating Theosophy. She also visited Asiatic countries and absorbed many Oriental ideas that were to appear later in her religious views.

In 1873 Madame Blavatsky arrived in the United States, where she became a citizen five years later. In the year of her arrival she met in Vermont one Colonel Olcott, a veteran of the Civil War and one who was to become her ardent disciple. She moved to New York, where her apartment became known as a "Lamasery"—the Tibetan word for a monastery. Before her death at sixty in 1891, she had published two books which have become standard works in Theosophy: *Isis Unveiled* and *The Secret Doctrine*.

The Theosophical Society. In September of 1875 an engineer named George Felt addressed seventeen persons on the subject, "The Lost Canon of Proportion of the Egyptians." The discussion that followed prompted General Alcott to suggest to Madame Blavatsky the formation of a society for the study and propagation of the occult—mysterious and magical aspects of religions. Within that year the Theosophical Society was founded—the same year in which Mary Baker Eddy published *Science and Health*. Permanent world headquarters have been established in Adyar, Madras, India—appropriately enough.

Annie Wood Besant (1847-1933). Successor to Madame Blavatsky in England was the brilliant wife of an Anglican clergyman. She was both an atheist and a divorcee, and H.P.B. had expressed some concern over her "psychic" adequacy. In the United States leadership passed, not to Colonel Olcott, but to one William Q. Judge. Olcott, it appears, was more an organizational loyalist than a perceptive "psychic."

Reports Walter R. Martin, "Among her many accomplishments, Mrs. Besant founded the Central Hindu College at Benares, India, in 1898, and also The Indian Home Rule League in 1916. In the year 1917 she was elected president of The Indian National Congress and was most always regarded as a powerful figure in Indian politics."[1]

Mrs. Besant announced in 1906 the arrival of the Messiah in the person of her adopted Indian son, Krishamurti. Many took this as truth, but by 1931 the son himself publicly rejected the title.

Thus it is that two women well versed in the sacred lore of India have put together the cult known today as Theosophy. Walter Martin estimates 12,000 select disciples.

Doctrines

God Is Impersonal. Like so many of the cults, Theosophy is a theological orphan—it has lost its Father. God to a Theosophist is but an impersonal principle filling all. Theosophy is pantheistic, it does not distinguish between Creator and creature. The end result of pantheism appears in this quotation from Mrs. Besant's adopted son, Krishnamurti, as preserved by Dr. Van Baalen: "For *you* are God, and you will only what God wills; but you must dig deep down into yourself to find the God within you, and listen to His voice, which is *your voice.*"[2]

Such a view of course contrasts radically with Christianity's very personal Father–God who counts hairs on the heads of His children and who calls them His own sons. A principle has no life in itself. It is merely a thought or concept. The God of Christians lives. He is a Person, not a principle (Matthew 16:16; John 6:57).

The Mahatmas. Where do the "revelations" originate which bring about the special truths of Theosophy? It is taught that a select group or highly developed spiritual or "psychic" persons are alive today and live in the Asian country of Tibet—long a land

---

[1]Walter R. Martin, *The Rise of the Cults*, p. 36.
[2]Jan Karl Van Baalen, *The Chaos of Cults*, p. 81.

of mystery. These enlightened persons are called *Mahatmas*. They could have decided to enter nirvana, the Theosophic equivalent of heaven, but they chose rather to remain in this world and channel the elect into Theosophic bliss. How does the world know their secret truths? That is easy—they simply chose Mrs. Blavatsky as their "agent." They revealed things to her; she in turn disclosed them to the waiting world.

Christians recognize the Bible alone as the sole authority for belief. For any schooled in evangelical Christianity, this strange teaching about the Mahatmas will appear more curious than convincing.

Seven-part Nature of Man. "The Theosophists have a peculiar doctrine of man. They assert that each individual is compounded of seven parts. The most common classification is the following: the physical body, the etheric double (or vital) body, the astral (or emotional) body, the mental body, the causal body, the future body, the perfected body. Salvation consists in moving from body to body until perfection is reached in the seventh body. Successively, the unimportant parts of the self are sloughed off like the unwanted skins of a snake."[3]

This conception of man requires a belief in a doctrine of salvation by works. Progress from one body to another not only involves reincarnation, but it also requires sacrifice and self-imposed humiliation.

Reincarnation. One of the distinctive teachings of Theosophy, clearly showing its Oriental character, is its belief that people now in bodies existed previously in another state, as other individuals. Their status today, whether wretched or wellborn, is determined by the quality of the previous life.

This belief of Theosophy represents an attempt to explain evil by simply saying that all suffering is the result of past sins, done in some previous incarnation. There are, then, no innocent persons.

Heaven and Hell. The Theosophical conception of heaven parallels that of Buddhism. A state called "nirvana" is finally reached after many reincarnations. In this state the individual is absorbed by the impersonal world soul, the un-Biblical God-spirit. He loses personal consciousness. "The theosophists also have their 'hell,' which oddly enough resembles the Catholic purgatory with indescribable tortures thrown in for good measure. 'Kamaloka,'

[3]Horton Davies, *The Challenge of the Sects*, pp. 36, 37.

which is the name for this intermediate state of existence, contains departed souls who suffer for their past sins awaiting reincarnation, or the chance to start living in a new body. . . ."[4] Obviously, such views are far from those of the Bible.

Evaluation

1. *Theosophy is an example of a gnostic cult.* It stresses secret truths mysteriously conveyed through enlightened intellects. The mind of course is involved in belief, according to Christianity, but the mysteries of the gospel are open secrets available to all.

2. *Theosophy is a mixture of many religions.* It proposes to link all faiths, giving common basis for a universal religion. Such a goal may be appreciated in view of the division in the world, but no true unity may be achieved where the words of Christ are not accepted without question.

3. *Theosophy denies the major doctrines of Christianity.* Its teaching as such would seriously impair the Christian understanding of God, Christ, sin, salvation, prayer, and atonement. Of the cults treated in this book, this is one of the most distant from Christianity.

BAHA'ISM

History

The Herald. In May of 1844, the same year in which the followers of William Miller awaited the visible return of the Lord according to their revised date, a twenty-five year old Persian man announced himself to his countrymen as a great prophet. Named Mirza Ali Mohammed, he took the title *the Bab,* which signifies "the Gate." Putting himself in the same class as Moses, Zoroaster, and Mohammed he foretold the impending arrival of a great prophet who would bring in a new era.

The Founder. The "Bab" was martyred at thirty-one years of age. The promised prophet appeared in the person of Mirza Husayn Ali, whom the Baha'is recognize as the founder of their religion. He took the name of Baha'u'llah, which means "the glory of God." Jesus said "the Son of man shall come in the glory of his Father" (Matthew 16:27). The Baha'is figure this prophecy was fulfilled in the coming of Baha'u'llah. The founder died in 1892—just a year after Charles Fillmore came upon the word *unity!*

---

[4]Martin, *op. cit.,* p. 38.

The Interpreter. The mantle of leadership passed to Baha'u'-llah's oldest son, Abdu'l-Baha, whose mission it was to interpret the many writings and teachings of Baha'u'llah the founder. During 1911 to 1914 he toured Europe and North America interpreting the Baha'i faith as he went. He was apparently an able apologist and won many converts.

The Guardian. When Abdu'l-Baha died in 1921, his grandson—Shoghi Effendi—took the reins of the movement. By the time of his death in 1957, the Baha'i faith was well established.

Status. Statistics available in 1961 indicate that the Baha'i faith has used 130 languages to reach 260 countries in the world. Five thousand localities have places of worship. Four temples are built, including the magnificent nine-sided one in Wilmette, suburban Chicago, and the international headquarters in Haifa, Israel.

Doctrines

All religions are one. The basic unity of all humanity and, therefore, all religions, rests as the foundation tenet of the Baha'i faith. And this teaching readily suggests the next.

Revelation is progressive. Here is an official statement from Baha'i literature:

> The fundamental principle enunciated by Baha'u'llah. . .is that religious truth is not absolute but relative, that Divine Revelation is a continuous and progressive process, that all the great religions of the world are divine in origin, that their basic principles are in complete harmony, that their aims and purposes are one and the same, that their teachings are but facets of one truth, that their functions are complimentary, that they differ only in the non-essential aspects of their doctrines, and that their missions represent successive stages in the spiritual evolution of human society.[5]

Christ is now replaced by Baha'u'llah. Each of the founders, Baha'is teach, was God's voice for his day. With the arrival of the "Glory of God" in the person of Baha'u'llah, a new day dawned and the dispensation of Jesus passed. It is not that these former teachers are of no permanent effect: they each have rather been superseded by a larger and fuller revelation.

Baha'u'llah fulfills Old Testament prophecy. One of the surprising features of Baha'ism appears in their pamphlet *Prophecy Fulfilled,* by Elisabeth H. Cheney. This booklet attempts to validate the Baha'i faith by showing it to be a fulfillment of Old Testament prophecy. Using the same line of reasoning as William

---

[5]Shoghi Effendi, *The Faith of Baha'u'llah* (Wilmette, Illinois: Baha'i Publishing Trust, 1959), p. 5.

Miller, the forerunner of the Seventh-day Adventists—and pointing to the same passage of Scripture, Daniel 8:13, 14—the author sees a marvelous fulfillment in the arrival of "the Bab" in 1844—same year as Miller's adjusted date of the Lord's predicted return.[6]

Evaluation

1. *Baha'ism may well be the coming cult.* By stressing the oneness of mankind and devaluing doctrinal differences, it creates an atmosphere friendly to current international, political, economic, and social goals. No one leaves anything; he simply adds an overarching interpretive religion.

2. *But Baha'ism stands at odds with Biblical Christianity.* As Walter Martin points out, either Christ is Lord of all or He is not Lord at all.[7] Baha'ism ignores redemption through Christ. The common Biblical definitions of God as a loving Father, of sin as a real and devastating power of evil, of the urgency for personal repentance and full-souled commitment to Jesus Christ alone as Lord—these ideas have evaporated from Baha'ism.

ZEN BUDDHISM

History

Origin. Buddhism is one of the major world religions today. There is a rising interest in Zen Buddhism apparent in America today. Few are aware that there is an association of Buddhist churches in America. For this reason this religion is studied here as a cult, even though it properly belongs in a study of world religions.

Ancient India was the source of this religion. Several features of that Indian culture persist in the Buddhist religion: belief in the reincarnation of souls, acceptance of many gods rather than one God, strange ideas of self-humiliation.

Guatama Buddha (563-483 B.C.?) The founder of Buddhism was born in a wealthy family and lived around the time of Jeremiah and Ezekiel. He was married and had a son, but he left his comfortable surroundings to seek an answer to the deep problems of life. The answer came, it is reported, as he reclined beneath a tree while meditating. Illumination arrived, so ever after he was known as the *Buddha,* which means "the enlightened

[6] Elisabeth H. Cheney, *Prophecy Fulfilled* (Wilmette, Illinois: Baha'i Publishing Trust, 1957), pp. 6–8.

[7] Martin, *op. cit.*, p. 119.

one." After his discovery, he traveled about taking what food interested people offered him and teaching the views he had come to adopt.

Divisions. Two divisions of Buddhism developed. *Mahayana* Buddhism stressed the likelihood that all persons would be saved due to the supposed sacrificial ministry of certain individuals—similar to the Mahatmas of Theosophy—who relinquished further development in order to assist those not so well advanced. *Hinayana* Buddhism, on the other hand, taught that each one must work out his own deliverance. The word *Zen* means meditation, and *Zen Buddhism* emphasizes that method.

Status. Buddhism spread through Asia covering Ceylon, Indonesia, Nepal, Tibet, China, Korea, and Japan. The 1962 *Yearbook of American Churches* lists an inclusive enrollment in the United States of 20,000 persons. American Buddhism is largely confined to Japanese-American people.

Teachings

Karma. The Buddhist method of salvation is called karma. "Karma may be described as the sum of an individual's thoughts and actions in all his previous incarnations. In each incarnation, he modifies his karma for either good or bad. . . . Karma can be bettered by good moral deeds, ritual, and ascetic self-discipline. The ultimate aim is not only to improve one's karma, but to do more, namely, to escape from the endless series of changes, the appalling eternal succession of births and rebirths. This would be salvation."[8]

The Four Basic Truths. Gautama Buddha taught his views in a simple summary. The hopeless reincarnation pattern could be broken if certain virtues were cultivated and actions taken. Here is a brief summary of his "four truths":

1. Human existence automatically involves suffering.
2. Suffering is caused by the desire for pleasure.
3. Release comes only through extinguishing the desire for pleasure.
4. An "eightfold path" must be followed to drive out pleasure.

The Eightfold Path. The way of salvation in Buddhism is traced by Buddha's eight steps:

1. Right views—The correct ones are the four listed above.
2. Right aspirations—Renounce pleasure; desire good.
3. Right speech—Don't lie; don't use idle words.

---

[8]Kenneth S. Latourette, *Introducing Buddhism* (New York: Friendship Press, 1956), p. 4.

4. Right conduct—Behave yourself.

5. Right vocation—Don't sell people as slaves or butcher animals.

6. Right effort—Cultivate positive states of mind.

7. Right mindfulness—Master yourself in every respect.

8. Right concentration—Meditate till peace comes.

Nirvana. The goal toward which the Buddhist strives is a place where the desire for pleasure—the cause of suffering—is eliminated. This state is called nirvana. It is not clear that this involves death itself, but it does entail the elimination of all improper striving for pleasure. This is the Buddhist equivalent of heaven.

Evaluation

1. *Acceptance of Buddhism in America indicates the search of modern man for peace.* Other Oriental religions are coming into the United States. A Mohammedan mosque recently was dedicated in the nation's capital. This tendency is increasing. American religious tolerance paves the way to future developments.

2. *The Oriental cults stand clearly opposed to Christianity.* The religion of Jesus stems directly from His words, among which were distinctive claims of His own deity. The Oriental religions proceed on the assumption that there are many gods and many sons of gods.

3. *The Oriental cults are pessimistic.* They are without hope in this world. They have no Book of Revelation guaranteeing God's final and complete conquest of evil.

FOR FURTHER READING

A standard account of Theosophy is found in *The Theosophical Movement: 1875-1925* (Dutton, 1925). Ironically, the headquarters of The Theosophical Society are in Wheaton, Illinois—a city otherwise known for its concentration of evangelical forces.

Walter R. Martin's *The Rise of the Cults* makes a good starting point for Baha'ism. Then use their booklets cited in the text by name.

Dr. D. T. Suzuki, best modern authority of Buddhism, has written the rather advanced book *An Introduction to Zen Buddhism* (Philosophical Library, 1949). *The Challenge of the Cults* (Zondervan, 1961) has a chapter of careful criticism by a Christian who is also a native Chinese.

FOR DISCUSSION

1. Do you see any common features in the Oriental cults?
2. What connection is there between Theosophy and Spiritualism?
3. What accounts for the appeal of the Baha'i faith?
4. What brings Zen Buddhism to American shores?
5. Contrast the Oriental nirvana with the Biblical heaven.

CHAPTER X

"Lords Many"

Minor Cults

There are less than ten groups that can be called major cults. They are "major" in the sense that they are generally known—even though a detailed knowledge of their teachings may be lacking.

In addition to these larger and better-known groups there are a number of smaller groups of lesser influence. These smaller groups are not less important, nor less significant. Indeed, to someone who has encountered any one of them, the word *minor* will be surprising. For any cult is major if it presents a serious challenge to the claims of the gospel.

We cannot possibly survey all the cults and isms. Like kingdoms, they rise and fall frequently. But in this chapter we select a group of some of the more common minor cults. The survey will necessarily be rapid, but the essence of each group will emerge clearly.

First Timothy 4:1-9 has some arresting information about recent isms. The first verse declares that there will be in the latter times those who depart (the Greek says, "apostasize") from the faith. This will take place through paying attention to "spirits" that beguile. There are, according to this passage, devilish doctrines. Notice these departures from the faith operate in the spiritual plane: the "spirits" deceive, it is "the Spirit" who foretells the apostasy. Because many heed such deceptive spirits, a wide range of religions and doctrinal allegiances develop. "There be gods many," said the Apostle Paul, "and lords many" (I Corinthians 8:5).

ANGLO-ISRAELISM

History

Not a Religion. Those who represent this group would be the first to claim that Anglo-Israelism is not any new religion. It is rather a theory held by persons of several Christian denominations. Some estimates claim two million adherents, but these figures cannot be verified.

In short, the theory of Anglo-Israelism, as implied in the name, is that the Anglo-Saxon countries—Great Britain and America—are the ten lost tribes of Israel.

Origin. As early as the year 1694 a writer by the name of John Sadler wrote a book linking ancient Israel with Britain. In 1840 John Wilson produced *Our Israelitish Origin*, and in 1871 Edward Hines penned the long title *The Identification of the British Nation with the Lost Tribes of Israel*. By 1879 the first Anglo-Saxon Association was formed in England. In the earlier days of the movement, the British Empire alone was considered. Later, America was brought into the theory.

Doctrines

Essence. Horton Davies offers a compact survey of the curious theory of British-Israelism. As a basis for his study, Dr. Davies used two pamphlets of the group: *Britain's Place in Prophecy,* by Commander Studd, and *The Heritage of the Anglo-Saxon Race,* by M. H. Gaylor. "From a perusal of these expositions, it appears that British-Israelites hold three basic beliefs. Firstly, they maintain that the Old Testament prophecies made by God to Abraham and confirmed to his descendants must be literally and materially fulfilled. In the second place, they hold that these promises and subsequent prophecies require for their fulfillment a belief that the ten tribes of the northern kingdom of Israel must have persisted as a nation, ruled by a king of the Davidic dynasty. Thirdly, they claim that Britain, the British Empire, and the United States of America, are the inheritors of the promises of God because they are the descendants of the ten lost tribes of Israel, and because Britain is ruled by a monarch of the Davidic line."[1]

Implication. Such a view of prophecy will of course appear strange to those who look for future fulfillments of prophecy to Israel itself. And it implies that the Western world is some sort of superior race greatly blessed of God.

Evaluation

1. *British-Israelism hopes to establish the truth of the Bible by these theories.* They do not oppose the Bible directly, but think

---

[1]*The Challenge of the Sects,* pp. 123, 124. My debt to this splendid little volume will appear especially evident in this chapter.

they are upholding its truthfulness by such a view. But this is doing a right thing in a wrong way.

2. *Were the ten tribes ever "lost"?* Anglo-Israelism is based on the assumption they were. Lamenting the many volumes of British-Israelite literature on the subject, Frank Boyd remarks "All the effort to write these volumes might well have been saved on the premise that 'they were never lost,' which we believe to be the correct one."[2]

3. *British-Israel teachings rest on disputable linguistic claims.* *British* for example is taken to stem from the Hebrew word *berith*, meaning covenant, and *ish*—meaning man. So *British* means a man of the covenant, according to the theory. The tribal name *Dan* is held to be found in the words *Dan*kirk and Lon*don*. But these arguments have no ample basis in linguistic scholarship and are based on coincidences only.

ASTROLOGY

History

Origin. Like Spiritualism, astrology—the belief that the position of the planets determines human fortunes—has a long history. There are a number of references in the Bible to astrologers—none approving the practice. Especially do the astrologers appear in the story of Daniel as those who could not equal his divinely given ability to interpret the dreams of the king. (Daniel 2:27, 28).

In Babylonia, or Chaldea, ancient observers noted the existence of fixed and "wandering" stars—the planets. The sun provided heat and light so essential to life. The moon determined the months and had effects on the tides. So the Chaldean scientists concluded that the heavenly bodies directly control human affairs. They developed an imaginary belt in the heavens called the *zodiac*, which was divided into twelve divisions—one for each month. Using the month for which one was born, an astrologer claims to be able to forecast future events by drawing a *horoscope* —a chart of planets in their relative position at a particular juncture.

Modern Astrology. There is a sense in which modern astrologers outdo ancient ones: "The Babylonians, at least, thought that superhuman beings directed the stars, which in turn guided the lives of individuals. Our present-day astrologers want us to accept

---

[2]Frank M. Boyd, *Book of the Prophet Ezekiel* (Springfield, Missouri: Gospel Publishing House, 1951), p. 166.

something even more preposterous—that stars without gods rule our national and personal destinies."[3]

Doctrines

Essence. We again have Horton Davies to thank for a neat sum of astrological belief: "What, then, is the nature of astrology? It is the belief that the planets and the stars exert a powerful and profound influence on the course of human events, both national and personal. The astrologer claims that by noting the exact positions of the planets and stars at the moment of the individual's birth he can give valuable information as to that person's character and probable destiny."[4]

Implication. Astrology makes no direct attack upon Christian theology. But it houses a view of the fixed determination of events which operates apart from the Biblical idea of a sovereign, personal God at the helm of the universe who can and does answer prayer.

Evaluation

1. *Astrology is superstitious and pagan.* It is Godless. It leaves no room for faith in an interested God vitally concerned with the course of history. It tends toward fatalism.

2. *The predictions of various astrologers disagree.* If the events were determined by the location of the planets at a given time, why do conflicting views arise?

3. *Dr. Van Baalen cites twins as a rebuttal of the claims of astrology.* Quite often they turn out differently. If born at the same time, would not their "signs" under the zodiac be alike?

4. *"The calculations of previous generations of astrologers have been discredited by the discovery of three planets since 1781."* Dr. Davies' incisive criticism is devastating. He continues: "How, we have a right to demand, could astrologers accurately predict the influence of planets on human affairs when they were unaware of the existence of three of eight already known to exist?"[5]

FATHER DIVINE

History

Birth. Somewhere around 1880, on Hutchinson Island in the Savannah River in Georgia, a lad was born to poor Negro share-

[3]Davies, *op. cit.*, p. 154.
[4]*Ibid.*, p. 152.
[5]*Ibid.*, pp. 155, 156.

cropper farmers. Few would ever dream that George Baker, as he was named, would some day be worshiped as God.

The Gardener. George Baker made his way to Baltimore where he began as a gardener. He was a Baptist, member of a Negro Baptist church. In Baltimore he met one Samuel Morris, an itinerant preacher. By a frightful misapplication of I Corinthians 3:16—"Ye are the temple of God"—George Baker came to believe he actually was God and possessed the authority of God. Samuel Morris encouraged him in this belief. The two were joined about 1908 by "Rev. St. John the Divine Hickerson." These three, Walter R. Martin suggests, "were the most colorful trio ever to have graced the unfortunate city of Baltimore."[6] Thus began Baker's belief that he was God.

About 1912 the trio split, however. There would be no Trinity. Baker was now using the titles "The Messenger," "God in the Sonship Degree," and Father Jehovia [sic]." The man who claimed to be God went south. In 1914 at Valdosta, Georgia, he was arrested but refused to give his real name. The court writ, Walter Martin reports, read thus: "The People *versus* John Doe, *alias* God."

New York City. About 1915, Father Divine came to New York City, soon to settle in Sayville, Long Island, in a dominantly white community. He began here to develop the lavish free banquets which betokened the bountiful provisions of the "Heavenly Father" he was claiming to be. Nobody, not even the Bureau of Internal Revenue, knows where all his money comes from.

The Death of Judge Smith. Residents of Sayville roundly objected to the strange activities in the "heaven" of Father Divine. In the early summer of 1932 Father Divine was brought to trial on charges of creating a public nuisance. The presiding judge, who was obviously opposed to the Father, was Supreme Court Justice Lewis J. Smith. Judge Smith refused leniency and sentenced Father Divine to a humiliating year in jail and a five hundred dollar fine. The sentence was passed on Saturday. The following Wednesday Judge Smith suffered a heart attack and died. He had been in good health. Commented Father Divine, "I hated to do it."

Unsavory Reports. Details may be found elsewhere (see the chapter in Martin's *The Rise of the Cults*), but there are sordid reports of sexual misbehavior on the part of the black Father

---

[6]*The Rise of the Cults*, p. 90.

with some of his white "angels." This is the more startling when we realize that in his pronouncements Father Divine expressly condemns participation in the sexual phase of marriage. His "converts" are instructed to sleep in separate rooms. In addition to this, as Dr. Martin points out, Father Divine from about 1930 to 1940 had close relations with the Communist party, though by 1950 he officially opposed it.

Doctrines

There is basically but one doctrine in the cult of Father Divine. It is the most blasphemous teaching imaginable: Father Divine claims he is God incarnated. "We believe," Dr. Martin heard over the telephone from one of Father's secretaries, "Father Divine to be the Godhead incarnate in the flesh—Father, Son, and Holy Spirit."

Evaluation

No refutation of the claims of Father Divine are needed. His claims need merely to be exposed to be condemned. The whole movement is absolutely astonishing and incredible, unless we believe the Scriptural prophecy of devilish doctrines and deceptive spirits abroad in the world. (I Timothy 4:1). The claim of a Negro gardener to be God in the flesh is surely the zenith of blasphemy.

ROSICRUCIANISM

History

Ancient. Similar to Moral Re-Armament, Unity, and Astrology, Rosicrucianism is not an organized religion. It is rather a fraternal fellowship akin to Masonic orders. Most ancient claims carry the movement back to ancient Egypt, to Thutmose III in 1489 B.C. Other historical accounts trace the origin of this brotherhood to a man, whether legendary or real, named Christian Rosenkreuz. He is supposed to have lived in the fourteenth or fifteenth century.

Modern. There are today two chief groups claiming to represent the ancient teachings of the Rosicrucians—both with headquarters in California. One group headquarters in Oceanside—the Rosicrucian Fellowship. The other group bears the impressive title, "Ancient Mystical Order Rosae Crucis"—commonly abbreviated AMORC. This group is especially insistent upon its claims to originality and authenticity. One of its pamphlets ends with a note: "There is but one international Rosicrucian Order operating throughout the world. . . . This organization does not sponsor a few modern publishing houses, or book propositions, operation under similar names, or selling instructions or books under the name of Rosicrucian fellowship, society, fraternity, and other similar titles."[7] Thus Rosicrucianism is itself a house divided.

The Rosy Cross. The name of the alleged founder, Christian Rosenkreuz, as well as the word *Rosicrucianism*, each contain the linguistic equivalent of "the rosy [or red] cross." The mystical symbol of this fraternal group envisions a cross representing man with arms outstretched upon which appears a rose as a symbol of chaste purity. A popular Rosicrucian greeting is, "May the Roses bloom upon your cross"—apparently a wish for increased perfection.

Doctrines

The Rosicrucians are a mystical brotherhood offering to members alleged secret knowledge that will result in unbelievable conquests and self-mastery. It is difficult to extract a full statement of their beliefs, since these are restricted as private valuable information. The views parallel those of Theosophy—including reincarnation.

A few extracts from a Rosicrucian pamphlet give the spirit and goals of the movement: "This is the mystical Way to Happiness, Success, and Peace Profound. . . . It is, truly, the SECRET KEY to material advancement and joy on earth, as well as to spiritual or mystical happiness to the universal consciousness [p. 7]. Free from creeds and sectarian dogmatism, tolerant and kindly, supporting no worldly redeemer and anticipating no Saviour other than God within man, the ROSICRUCIAN ORDER, AMORC, opens its portals to all and invites the unknowing and the seeking, to tarry in the consoling retreats of mystical knowledge and regenerated life" [p. 9].[8]

Evaluation

So obvious a Scripture passage as John 3:16 clearly indicates to those whose belief is founded on the Bible that the sole requirement for eternal life is belief. Biblical belief means commitment,

---

[7]*Why Are We Here? And Why Are Our Lives Unequal?* (San Jose, California: The Rosicrucian Press, Ltd., 1952), p. 10.

[8]*Am I My Brother's Keeper: The Law of Karma* (San Jose, California: The Rosicrucian Press, n.d.).

not discovery of a secret. Once again Galatians 1:8, 9 are appropriate verses to apply. They are Paul's curse upon anyone who proclaims another message than the one God revealed to Paul—the gospel of Jesus Christ.

SWEDENBORGIANISM
History

Emanuel Swedenborg (1688-1772). This Swedish government official is widely recognized as a genius and scholar of the first rank. A life-long bachelor, he was an accomplished scientist—having produced more than thirty sizable volumes on subjects ranging from metallurgy to physiology. He anticipated the invention of the airplane and the submarine. Later in life, his interests turned to theology and plunging into the subject he produced another thirty volumes in that field. To this day the Swedenborgian church stresses the importance of careful study—especially of Swedenborg's writings.

Robert Hindmarsh. A London printer, Hindmarsh brought together a group of persons for the purpose of discussing Swedenborg's works. In this way the "New Church," as the Swedenborgian church is more properly called, was formed. Swedenborg himself had done no preaching and, though convinced of a forthcoming restoration of the church, did not himself initiate the new organization. The first American church was formed in Baltimore in 1792.

Status. For their age, the Swedenborgian church is not growing with any vigor. Current estimates of their total membership vary between 6,000 and 11,000—with a possible world membership of 30,000.

Doctrines

Special Revelations Through Emanuel Swedenborg. These constitute a basic assumption of the New Church. Their pamphlet, *What is a Swedenborgian?*, by William F. Wunsch, credits Swedenborg with visions of the other world which constitute a source for much of his teaching.[9]

A Special Interpretation of the Trinity. The same pamphlet describes the Trinity, which doctrine the New Church says it accepts, in this way: "In the one God the Lord, the Savior Jesus Christ, there is, a depth of being known only to Himself, and this is God 'the Father'; In Him is God visible to thought and

[9]William F. Wunsch, *What Is a Swedenborgian?* (Chicago: The Swedenborg Press, n.d.), p. 5.

manifested to men, and this is 'the Son'; and in Him is God imparting of Himself, the holy Spirit."[10]

Second Coming Fulfilled in Swedenborg. Their *Handbook of General Information* is quite blunt: "The Lord's Second Coming was accomplished by means of a man, His servant Emanuel Swedenborg, whom He filled with His Spirit and called to teach the doctrines of the New Church, through the Word, from Him."[11] The Second Coming is therefore now under way.

Evaluation

Swedenborgianism is similar to Seventh-day Adventism in the high position accorded to gifted seers standing at the origin of their movements. Like SDA, Swedenborgianism wishes to be understood as standing within the limits of Christianity, rather than outside as a heresy. But traditional Christianity has looked askance at claims to "special truths" by any prophet which appear to add to the common core of teaching that can be traced from apostolic days and that is not disturbed by varying emphases of the denominations.

For Further Reading

Primary sources for these groups are less readily accessible. Dr. Van Baalen's book, *The Chaos of Cults* (Eerdmans, 1962) has chapters on each of the groups discussed in this book, except on Father Divine. For a satisfying survey of Father Divine, see Chapter VII of Walter R. Martin's *The Rise of the Cults* (Zondervan, 1955).

For Discussion

1. Express in a sentence the essence of the teachings of these groups.
2. To what would you attribute Father Divine's astounding success?
3. Is there anything secret about the gospel? anything mysterious? What is the difference?
4. Does scholarship guarantee correctness?

---

[10]*Ibid.*, p. 6.
[11]*The General Church of the New Jerusalems A Handbook of General Information* (Bryn Athyn, Pennsylvania: The Academy Book Room, 1952), p. 6.

CHAPTER XI

The Vast Vatican

Roman Catholicism

The groups considered thus far are those commonly regarded as non-Christian cults. In this chapter and the next, we are going to review two prominent features of American religion which are not properly called cults. Roman Catholicism and modernism are nominally Christian: they both profess to represent the Christian religion in its most satisfactory form (this is not true, however, of humanism—an extreme form of modernism).

The ordinary Christian believer is more likely to come into contact with a Roman Catholic or a modernist than he is with an ardent member of one or other of the cults. Both Roman Catholicism and modernism are, from an evangelical standpoint, defective forms of Christianity. They are included in this book since they represent departures from the center of evangelical Christianity and since their total influence even exceeds that of the non-Christian cults.

Roman Catholicism presents one of the most serious of all challenges to the true Christian faith. The Roman church is a curious combination: it guards with utmost care such basic Christian doctrines as the virgin birth, deity, and resurrection of Christ. It argues effectively for the truth of the Trinity. But in addition to these fundamental doctrines which are tenaciously held, the Roman church adds numerous teachings which cut at the heart of the religion of true grace. This is the real threat of Catholicism: orthodox blessings and heretical cursings proceed out of the same theological mouth.

It is important to achieve a clear understanding of the history of the Roman Catholic church in order to challenge its claim to authority.

HISTORY

Origin

The Catholic Claim. An issue of crucial importance in under-standing the Catholic church is its claim to have been founded by Jesus Christ Himself. The appendix in *Father Smith Instructs Jackson,* a standard explanation of the Catholic faith, sets forth the "Date of Origin of the Principal Churches in the United States." The list looks something like this, of course with many more churches mentioned:[1]

Name	Place of Origin	Founder	Year
Adventists	Dresden N. J.	William Miller	1831
Friends	England	George Fox	1648
Lutherans	Germany	Martin Luther	1517
Mennonites	Holland	Menno Simons	1525
United Brethren	Susquehanna Valley	William Otterbein	1766

This is a handy and accurate chart of the founding of several prominent denominations. But at the very top of the list and, unlike the others, printed with boldface capital letters, appears this line:

CATHOLIC CHURCH   JERUSALEM   JESUS CHRIST   33

This is a subtle and offensive claim. It gives the impression that the existing structure of the Roman Catholic church was alone founded by Jesus Christ and that all the other churches are recent arrivals on the scene of history and are without any connection to the church Jesus founded.

The Denomination and the Church. Actually, the dates given for the origin of the various bodies are the dates of the founding of the *denomination.* One of the primary Roman Catholic errors is to confuse the *church* with the *denomination.* The *church,* by Biblical definition, is the invisible body of believers of whatever age and whatever denominational relationship who are in true and living relationship with Jesus Christ. A *denomination,* on the other hand, is a visible organization of a group of Christians hold-ing similar views who have formed an organization in order to carry out the work of witnessing the gospel as they see it.

The Biblical idea of the church, the called group of believers, and the earthly organization of the denomination are not neces-sarily one and the same. Rome says they are; therefore, there can be but one true church—the Roman Catholic church. But any denomination reflects the church only to the extent that it fulfills

---

[1]John Francis Noll and Lester J. Fallon, *Father Smith Instructs Jackson* (Huntington, Indiana: Our Sunday Vistory Press, 1960), p. 225.

the teachings and purposes of Jesus. Every denomination, therefore, that truly offers the gospel of Christ may be understood as
having its real origin with Christ.

It is true that nothing is said of denominations in the Bible.
But this is as true for Roman Catholicism as for the many denominations of Protestantism. Denominations exist for the sake
of the church. Denominations are organizations, the church is an
organism. Hell will likely be heavily populated with "members of
denominations." Heaven will contain only members of the church,
"which is his body."

Date of Origin. When therefore did Roman Catholicism originate? In its present form, Roman Catholicism is the result of a
thousand years of development after the initial origin of the
church founded by Jesus. Very important is the fact that in the
first thousand years or so of Christian history there was but one
church. Divisions were minor. Rome claims to be this one church.
But Catholicism more accurately preserves extensive developments within that one church—developments which were destined
to carry the church away from its glorious and holy origin.

We may allow Rome the claim that their church was founded
in A.D. 33 only if we clearly understand that what they have come
to be was certainly not begun by Jesus. Beginning in the second
to the fourth centuries, increasing in the following centuries,
and firmly established by the eleventh century (when the Eastern
Orthodox branch split off from Western, or Roman, Catholicism)
—Roman Catholicism with its current array of liturgy, hierarchy,
and non-Biblical doctrine hardly even has a "founding date."
It began, we must say, the moment meaningless liturgical acts
were substituted for personal worship.

Development

Rise of the Pope. Rome was the capital of the ancient world,
and it was natural that the leader of the church at Rome should
soon be elevated to church-wide leadership. This is how the office
of the pope originated. The word *pope* stems from a Latin word
which means "father, bishop." Protestants generally recognize
Gregory I as the first real pope. He ruled from A.D. 590-604.
Catholics claim Peter was the first pope, though the evidence
is not conclusive that Peter was ever in Rome. Increasingly, the
pope's office expanded from a spiritual director of a local con-
gregation to a powerful political influence over the whole of
medieval Europe.

Development of Liturgy. As enthusiastic personal religion gradually co-operated, preaching was replaced by the Mass—a distortion of the communion service in which the sacrifice of Christ on Calvary is dramatically re-enacted. Monks, nuns, and monasteries arose and liturgy was elaborated as a fine art.

Spiritual Decay. The Middle Ages were not without living lights of the gospel, and many a Catholic saint was a true saint of God as well. The popes, even, were not all evil or mercenary. But the prevailing trend of spiritual life was downward through the period when the Roman Catholic church was gaining increasing prominence and influence.

Reformation. By the sixteenth century, the state of religion had reached a tragic low. A gifted young man was earnestly concerned—enough to forsake studies in law to enter a Catholic monastery in preparation for the priesthood. This monk, Martin Luther, discovered personally—then shared with the world—the long-obscured truth that we are saved not by what we do, but by what God did. Out of this priest's revolt, Protestantism was born.

Expanding Doctrine. A fundamental plank in Rome's thinking is the progressive nature of doctrine. Doctrine, in the Roman view, is not determined alone by the Bible; the church has the power to interpret the Bible and add theological statements which are found in the Bible only in "germ" form. This explains why Catholics believe that the pope speaks infallibly when defining doctrine, or that Mary was taken bodily into heaven and had no sin of her own.

Current Status

Statistics on the wide achievements, the many thousands of Catholic educational activities, the millions of dollars worth of properties, and the world-wide influence of the Roman Catholic church would fill a fair-sized almanac. But a few cold and hard facts about Roman Catholicism are sobering enough. Here they are (1961 figures):

—9% of the world's 2.8 billion people are Roman Catholics. This is the largest single Christian segment. The Moslems represent 15% and Hindu 12%. Only 8% are Protestant.

—Roman Catholic membership in the United States approaches 41 millions, making that church the largest single group of Christians in the United States. All Protestants put together total over 62.5 millions, the largest single Protestant church being the Methodist Church, with nearly 10 million members.

—During the decade from 1950 to 1960 Roman Catholicism experienced a growth rate of close to 50% as opposed to an average growth factor of about 33%. Cautions Harold Lindsell: ". . .if its rate of growth continues without equal Protestant growth, the Roman Church will eventually become the dominant force in American life."[2]

DOCTRINES

Roman Catholicism is surprisingly orthodox: they accept and defend such basic doctrines as the deity of Christ, His literal resurrection, the Holy Trinity—and others. But certain teachings drawn from tradition rather than from the Bible distinguish them from other Christians:

"The Bible Is NOT Our Sole Guide"

Description. This phrase is the title of a small booklet, one of many distributed broadly by the Knights of Columbus—an effective propaganda arm of the Roman Catholic church. Another pamphlet clearly states their opinion: "The New Testament writings were never meant to be the sole and final authority for Christ's revealed truth. They were never intended as the complete and only source of certain knowledge of Christian faith and duty. Prove it by the Bible? The Catholic Church proves it from what Christ and His Apostles taught. The Catholic Church was there to hear them and has held fast to their teaching."[3] The Bible, therefore, is the property of the church, and it cannot be interpreted by the ordinary man but must be accepted as interpreted by the officials of the Roman church down through history.

Response. Evangelical Christians believe that God's Word is the ultimate source of authority. They believe that this Word has been written down as the Bible. They believe each Christian has the right to go individually to the Scriptures to find God's will for his life. How can we learn of the authority of Christ or of God except we read of it in the Bible? We cannot trust Catholic "tradition," since it demands we believe many things not discoverable in Scripture itself and then we would not know just whose "tradition," to accept. There is such a thing, we learn in the Bible, as "making the word of God of none effect through your tradition" (Mark 7:13).

Mary, the Mother of God

Description. Catholics give to Mary the mother of Jesus the highest form of veneration to which any "saint" is entitled. Popu-

---

[2]Lindsell, *et al.*, p. 9.
[3]*The Bible is a Catholic Book* (Pamphlet number 3; St. Louis: Knights of Columbus—Religious Information Bureau, 1960), p. 18.

lar usage has made little difference between this degree of veneration and the worship due God, since prayers are addressed to her
as well as to God. Special attention was given to Mary in the
very early years of the church. Since she was, as Luke 1:28 indicates, "highly favored," it was easy to soon call her "the mother of
God"—which she was, in the sense that Christ is God. But Protestants have generally avoided the phrase because of the additional
meaning attached to the word by later Catholic dogma.

The Catholic doctrine of Mary has grown with history, a development encouraged by the Catholic belief that the church
has the right to expand doctrine apart from the Bible. In 1854, the
Pope announced the "Dogma of the Immaculate Conception,"
teaching "that the doctrine, which holds that the Most Blessed
Virgin Mary at the first moment of her conception was, by singular
grace and privilege of the Omnipotent God, in virtue of the
merits of Jesus Christ, Saviour of the human race, preserved from
all stain of original sin, is revealed by God, and therefore to be
firmly and resolutely believed by all the faithful."[4]

To this teaching that Mary, unlike all other humans, was
born without sin was added—by declaration of the Pope in 1950—
the "Dogma of the Assumption." Said the Pope: "We pronounce,
declare, and define it to be a divinely revealed dogma: that the
Immaculate [sinless] Mother of God, the ever Virgin Mary, having
completed the course of her earthly life, was assumed body and
soul into heavenly glory."

Response. This development in the doctrine of Mary demonstrates the Catholic policy of making the Church superior to
Scripture. There can be no more fundamental cleavage between
Catholicism and Bible-believing Protestantism. Where the Bible
says simply "highly favored," the Roman Catholic says "immaculate" and "assumed body and soul into heavenly glory." The next
logical step feared by many is the definition of Mary as "co-re-
demptrix" with Jesus Christ. To all this the Protestant can only
say that it does not "stand written."

The Infallible Pope

Description. Catholics do not believe that everything the Pope
says is incapable of being wrong. They believe that when the
pope speaks officially, in defining doctrine, he is infallible: "It is

4From the translation of the dogmatic pronouncement of Pope Pius IX made on December
8, 1854 and entitled "Ineffabilis Deus." Quoted in *The Radiant Crown* (New York:
The Paulist Press, 1953), p. 5.

a dogma divinely revealed that the Roman Pontiff when he speaks *ex cathedra,* that is when in discharge of the office of pastor and doctor of all Christians and by virtue of his supreme apostolic authority he defines a doctrine regarding faith or morals to be held by the Universal Church, is possessed of that infallibility with which the Divine Redeemer willed that His Church should be endowed for defining doctrine regarding faith or morals."[5]

Response. Evangelical Christians ascribe the impossibility of error to the Scriptures. Roman Catholics exchange them for the pope. Their doctrine accordingly can exceed Scripture, while evangelical doctrine must abide within the limits set by the Scriptures.

Other Catholic Beliefs and Practices

The materials listed in *For Further Reading* may be consulted for a fuller treatment of this brief list of distinctive Catholic views:

Purgatory. After death, departed souls undergo a purging—from which the word *purgatory* stems—in order to qualify for eternal life.

Mass. The Catholic Mass is a highly symbolical re-enactment of the sacrifice of Jesus. By the miraculous power of God, as the Catholics believe, the wine and the bread are transformed into the actual blood and body of the Lord.

Rosary. This aid to Catholic devotion consists of a string of fifty-nine beads, each of which represents the recital of a certain prayer. *Rosary* comes from *roses,* and suggests the formation of the beads as a garland of roses.

Crucifix. This is an image of the cross on which appears the figure of the crucified Christ. It is used in Catholic churches, institutions, and homes to remind Catholics of Christ's sacrifice.

EVALUATION

1. *Catholicism confuses the denomination with the church.* This becomes clear in the review of the history of the Catholic church. To members of Christ's Body—the Biblical Church—this is both an offensive and an arrogant claim. In the Bible the church is portrayed as a world-wide body of believers existing in visible local congregations. Membership in this Body was then, as now, secured by supernatural rebirth through the work of the Holy

---

[5] *A Short Story of the Popes* (Pamphlet number 11; St. Louis: Knights of Columbus—Religious Information Bureau, 1960), p. 39.

Spirit following repentance and belief on the part of the awakened believer. A man may be a member of the denomination without being a member of the church. And he may possibly be a member of the church without as yet having identified himself with any denomination. For Catholicism there is one church identified specifically with one denomination—the Roman Catholic church. But this view undercuts the whole conception of spiritual membership in the mystical Body of Christ.

On the level of the common man, Catholic doctrine is often interpreted to mean that salvation is obtained by joining the Roman Catholic church. But salvation is by faith alone (Ephesians 2:8, 9), and regeneration is a spiritual change brought about by the Holy Spirit (John 3:3–8; Titus 3:5). The church is not the source of salvation: it is the society of the saved. We are saved not *by* the church but *for* it.

2. *Catholics lower the importance of the Bible.* They place the denomination above the Bible, where they ought to hold the denomination under the searching authority of the Bible. Denominations may err; but the Bible is the Word of the all-knowing God. Catholics are taught they do not have the right to interpret the Scriptures for themselves. The Bible, they learn, is not easy to understand. When a Catholic reads the Bible, he must do it with the assistance of the standard interpretations laid down by the teaching church. In place of the authority Protestants ascribe to the Bible, Catholics substitute the pope.

Incidentally, the full official title of the pope is, "His Holiness the Pope, Bishop of Rome and Vicar of Jesus Christ, Successor of St. Peter, Prince of the Apostles, Supreme Pontiff of the Universal Church, Patriarch of the West, Primate of Italy, Archbishop and Metropolitan of the Roman Province and Sovereign of Vatican City."

3. *All true Christians are catholic.* The word *catholic* means universal. Members of Christ's Body are members of the universal church, that is, of the church that is found everywhere and in every era since its origin. The Apostles' Creed, used by Catholic and Protestant alike (since it comes from the period when there was but one church which was properly neither "Catholic" nor "Protestant") speaks of "one holy Catholic Church." Romanism calmly identifies itself with this "one holy Catholic church" and disregards all others. Every Christian is a "catholic" in the sense that he belongs to the "one holy Catholic church" which is the living Body of Christ.

4. *It is possible for a Roman Catholic to be a true Christian*. It is God who knows hearts. If there are true believers among them, it will be in spite of the distinctive teachings of Catholicism. The truth essential to salvation is available in Roman Catholicism, though that kernel is encrusted with many centuries of dogmatic additions and ritualistic practices. God is able, however, to find people of "every nation," as Peter had to learn of the Gentiles (Acts 10:35). But the ritualism and formalism of the Roman Catholic system do not suit the full and free proclamation of the gospel ordinarily enjoyed in the evangelical churches.

FOR FURTHER READING

First-hand sources on Catholicism are easy to come by. The able Knights of Columbus have for several years carried on an extensive advertising program. For seven cents each, one may get a variety of pamphlets on various topics. Number 50, *This is the Catholic Church*, makes a good one to start with and contains a list of about fifty other titles.

The free home study course offered by the Knights uses *Father Smith Instructs Jackson*, a 230 page paperback as a textbook. Another readable study of the Catholic faith is entitled *Life in Christ* (Chicago, 1958). It too is a paperback. Both these books are written in easy-to-understand language and are definitely in the class of propaganda.

Paul Blanshard, neither Catholic nor evangelical, has been a persistent critic of Catholicism. Beacon Press of Boston publishes his books, which include most notably *American Freedom and Catholic Power* (2nd ed., 1958), *The Irish and Catholic Power* (1953), and *Communism, Democracy, and Catholic Power* (1951). These have been controversial books, but they are stiff criticism.

From an evangelical standpoint George Salmon's *The Infallibility of the Church* has been standard since first published in 1888. There have been many editions by various publishers. It is currently published by Baker Book House. G. C. Berkouwer presents an advanced criticism in *The Conflict With Rome* (Presbyterian and Reformed, 1958) and Loraine Boettner offers in *Roman Catholicism* (Presbyterian and Reformed, 1962) a veritable encyclopedia of evangelical criticism of Romanism.

The Christian Heritage is a monthly magazine that deals specifically with Catholic issues from an evangelical standpoint. It is published by Christ's Mission, 369 Carpenter St., Sea Cliff, New York. This group can also supply useful literature and tracts on Catholicism.

FOR DISCUSSION

1. Why is it hard to say when Catholicism originated?
2. Why does Catholicism constitute a serious threat?
3. What is the true relationship of the church to the Bible?
4. What is the real meaning of the word *catholic*?

CHAPTER XII

Reason the Rudder
Modernism

One thing catapulted the middle ages into the modern era: the unrestricted supremacy of human reason—reason unrestrained either by church tradition or by a Biblical estimate of the nature of man and his universe, which properly constitute the subjects of the vast scientific revival that was about to break open.

Reason became the rudder, the guide to science. With reason as the rudder Columbus looked out, Galileo looked up, Freud looked in. With reason applied in science, invention, discovery, exploration, it looked like the world was about to enter a scientific millennium.

But a dilemma arose. For all the ways in which man had bettered his world, he had somehow been unable to cancel out evil. In fact, it worked the other way: as technology soared, evil intensified. Imagine! The early '40's of this, the *space* century, witnessed readers glaring at incredible newspaper reports of a grown, apparently sane man herding people into oversized ovens and gassing and baking them—just because they were Jews. Why, people had gotten to the place where they were talking about *world* wars, not just two-nation skirmishes. They even started numbering the world wars: two went by in a single generation. And we seem to be ever living on the lip of the third.

Was reason, the gentle servant, about to become reason, the over-powering rebel? Things called for a change, and change there has been. But this is not the place for an analysis of philosophical and theological reactions to recent history.[1]

We can, however, look briefly at some of the religious results of the reaction of reason on Christianity. These newer interpre-

---

[1]This has been done by Carl F. H. Henry in his two books *Remaking the Modern Mind* (Grand Rapids: Wm. B. Eerdman's Publishing Co., 1946) and *The Protestant Dilemma* (Grand Rapids: Wm. B. Eerdman's Publishing Co., 1948).

tations are generally gathered under the term *modernism,* though admittedly they do not all quite fit there.

Modernism in religion, then, is not so much a set of beliefs as it is a way of reaching beliefs. It is not a creed but a method. It begins whenever reason is crowned and tradition—either church-ly or Biblical—is submerged.

There is a sense in which even evangelical Christianity is modern:[2] it most carefully attempts to relate the teachings of the Bible to the present day, to modern times. Luther's break with Rome sharply contradicted accepted standards of doctrine but it was based on the then very "modern" idea of the superiority of the Bible's authority over that of the pope. Without that radical break there would have been no Protestantism. The word *modernism,* however, is commonly used to designate a specific group of conclusions necessarily opposed to certain basic evangelical doctrines.

A number of neighboring terms might appear confusing. *Modernism* stresses the willingness to adjust beliefs to the latest demands of recent—or "modern"—science. *Liberalism* means nearly the same thing but emphasizes freedom of inquiry. *Skepticism* doubts the possibility of discovering anything that can be positively identified as truth. *Biblical criticism* views the Bible as the result of literary editing and consequently lowers the uniqueness of the Bible. *Atheism* is an outright denial of the existence of God. Modernism, or liberalism, is often skeptical and occasionally atheistic, though not necessarily so. Even in Jesus' day there were modernists (Luke 20:27).

HUMANISM

The two poles of moral activity in the universe are God and man, deity and humanity. Christian theology has always stressed God, since it distrusted the fallen nature of man. The movement called humanism focuses the spotlight on man—his abilities, his potential. While humanism means different things at different times, it always centers in humanity, in man.

History

Roots. The roots of humanism strike back through history to the ancient classical world where in Greece and Rome voices pleaded for individualism and freedom from restraint. But the

---

[2]See President V. Raymond Edman's article, "Who is Today's True Liberal?" in the February, 1962, issue of the *Bulletin of Wheaton College,* Wheaton, Illinois.

greatest form of humanism arose along with the Renaissance, which occurred in the major countries of Europe between A.D. 1350 and 1650. The word itself means rebirth, and the Renaissance witnessed a revival of culture and learning.

Advance. Prior to the Renaissance, the Roman Catholic church had imposed restrictions on what material could be studied and even specified conclusions that must be reached. Humanism advanced during this period as men began to throw off the authority of the church and to think for themselves. For Protestantism, which also originated during this period, relief from the overbearing authority of the church provided the freedom to obey the Bible according to one's own conscience. But for the humanists, heeding the Bible was a sorry substitute for heeding the church; they threw both overboard.

Humanism Today. While humanism is not an organized movement, persons sympathizing with its ideas have persisted ever since. Applied to the field of religion, humanism seeks a "religion without God"—a religion in which personal satisfactions here and now crowd out Biblical demands for sacrifice and the Christian hope for a better future.

Doctrines

The Christian Century, a weekly magazine widely recognized as the voice of liberal Protestantism, reprinted some years ago, a document called "The Humanist Manifesto."[3] Interestingly enough, even the modernistic *Christian Century* found it impossible to approach this document in a "spirit of calm respect." The humanists, you might say, are even too modernistic for the modernists! From this "Manifesto," here are some points of belief.

1. *Evolution.* "7. Humanism believes that man is a part of nature and that he has emerged as the result of a continuous process."

2. *No Supernatural.* "5. Humanism asserts that the nature of the universe depicted by modern science make unacceptable any supernatural or cosmic guarantees of human values. . . . Religion must formulate its hopes and plans in the light of the scientific spirit and method."

3. *This-worldly.* "8. Religious humanism considers the complete realization of human personality to be the end of man's life, and seeks its development and fulfillment in the here and now."

4. *Prayer Replaced.* "9. In place of the old attitudes involved

---

[3]"The Humanist Manifesto," *The Christian Century*, June 7, 1933, pp. 743–745.

in worship and prayer the humanist finds his religious emotions expressions in a heightened sense of personal life and in a co-operative effort to promote social well-being."

5. *Economic Dissatisfaction.* "14. The humanists are firmly convinced that existing acquisitive and profit-motivated society has shown itself to be inadequate and that a radical change in methods, controls, and motives must be substituted."

Evaluation

The insistence of humanism that "man is the measure" of what is to be regarded as important neglects the Christian condemnation of human nature as sinful. How can sinful man determine what is best for him when even his mind suffered from the Fall? Humanism suggests a religion in which there is no God except man himself, no heaven except "well-being" here on earth, no sin except failure to progress. Without formal organization, this way of thinking threatens the church largely by filtering into society through humanist writers and educators.

UNITARIANISM AND UNIVERSALISM

Of the four movements discussed in this chapter only one has formally organized into a religious body. This one is the "Unitarian Universalist Association," which resulted from a recent merger of the Unitarian and Universalist churches. The very fact that this church has organized for positive action shows that these churches are not primarily negative—as they appear to be from an evangelical standpoint since their affirmations are so few and their denials strong. Universalists and Unitarians unshamedly use the word *liberal* in describing themselves. To them it is no loss, but a gain, to be released from the restrictive theological concepts commonly held by the orthodox churches.

History

Unitarian Backgrounds. While it has roots extending back to the early centuries of the church, Unitarianism as a modern movement began in Europe after the Reformation. The first Unitarian church in America was King's Chapel in Boston, an Episcopal church which had lost its rector and finally, in 1785, voted to become Unitarian. Twenty years later a Unitarian professor of theology was installed at Harvard, which had been founded a century and a half earlier for the training of orthodox ministers.

From then on Unitarianism grew, producing no less than five American presidents.

Universalist Backgrounds. Universalists too find their counterparts in the early years of Christian history. Their belief represents a logical development in an extreme reaction against Calvinism. They hold that salvation in the last day will be extended to everyone, that redemption is universal. Englishman John Murray brought the teaching to America about 1770.

Recent Merger. In May of 1961 the Unitarians and the Universalists merged to form one church. The ease of the union is not hard to explain. Both had remained comparatively small in spite of their rather lengthy existence. Both were perpetually dissatisfied with the approach and conservatism of traditional Christianity. Both affirmed the value of liberal religion. Both found favor in the upper social and intellectual levels. The merger put together the two groups who represent organized modernism. Figures supplied for the memberships of both bodies by the 1962 *Yearbook of American Churches* show a combined membership of approximately 175,000.

Doctrines

As true liberals, Unitarians and Universalists are not primarily interested in theology. Their members are given the widest latitude in selecting those beliefs which most appeal to them.

Unitarian Beliefs. The word *unitarian* hints at the basic interest of that movement: it stresses the unity of God, that there is but one God. Unitarians reject the common Christian conception of the Trinity. They do this because they give high place to reason, and the concept of a God who is three and one at the same time appears to them an impossible contradiction. Affirmation of God's unity is the essence of Unitarianism. To this is added a number of other beliefs similar to those described for Universalism below. Evangelicals would strongly protest the implication of the Unitarian idea of God: if God is one, and that One is not a Trinity, then Jesus must be seen as a man—a highly developed man, the world's great teacher—but still a man.

Universalist Beliefs. From a brochure offering universalism as an "Alternative to Orthodoxy," here are a few extracts clearly indicating their beliefs: " (2) Man is not a 'fallen' sinner needing to be saved by miraculous saviours; he is a struggling being striving to remove the attributes of his past. His 'salvation' will be accomplished by his own good works and as he comes to realize that wholeness is achieved through love, charity, justice, and freedom. (3) We view Jesus as a teacher of such ideals, a remarkable human being esteemed along with Gandhi, Buddha, Lincoln, and others. (5) The Bible is seen as one traditional point of view, not always accurate or inspirational. The Universalist selects from its pages what appears to him to be of worth and adds it to other writings, the large and ever-growing accumulation of which is his 'sacred' literature."[4]

Evaluation

It would not be difficult to gather together a huge number of Biblical texts showing that these beliefs do not correspond to the sense of Scripture. This would satisfy some, but the real difference is more basic. Unitarians and Universalists assume the ability of the human mind to seek and discover truth without outside supernatural assistance. The evangelical believer, on the other hand, assumes that the mind unaided is not capable of discovering the truth essential to eternal salvation. There is of course the inherent power of the Word of God in quoting Scripture passages. But the basic problem should be recognized as one turning on the fundamental question, what is the source of authority? Unitarians answer, human reason. Evangelicals answer, the Bible. Any witness to Unitarian Universalists must be alert to this fundamental division.

LIBERALISM

Religious or theological liberalism is generally a synonym for modernism, though some persons make tiny differences. Liberalism, or modernism, differs from humanism in that liberalism gives special pre-eminence to Christianity and to Christ, while humanism finds good in all faiths and finality in none. Liberalism differs from Unitarian-Universalism in that it is not formally organized like these groups. All Unitarians and Universalists are liberals, but not all liberals are Unitarians or Universalists. While liberals claim the name Christians, humanists would not wish to be so restricted. Humanists, therefore, are further away from traditional Christianity.

History

Friedrich D. E. Schleiermacher (1768-1834). This gentleman with the long German name rates the title "father of liberalism."

---

[4]*Universalism: Alternative to Orthodoxy* (Boston: Department of Extension, The Universalist Church of America, n.d.).

He was a German philosopher and theologian who taught that theology consists in interpreting religious experience. Experience comes first—then doctrine. This belief melted any objective test of doctrine and led to the typical liberal de-emphasis on theological statements.

Rise of Biblical Criticism. Increasingly through the eighteenth and nineteenth centuries, as modern men shook off external restraints of any sort, the Bible came under fire. Jean Astruc, a French physician, while doing research on Biblical medical laws concluded that books ascribed to Moses were in reality compiled editions of several individual writings written after the time of Moses. In time other theories were developed which resulted in depriving the Bible of its uniqueness, authority, and reliability. More recent research has reversed the trend and re-established the authentic character of the Bible. But the rise of Biblical criticism fed the emerging spirit of liberalism in Christianty.

Secularizing Forces in the Nineteenth Century. Several views contributed to the neglect of the Biblical view of man and his world. Charles Darwin in 1859 announced that man had evolved from lower animal forms. Sigmund Freud defined the sexual impulse as most basic to human nature. And Karl Marx argued for the revision of society on what were actually communistic principles. These and other influences forced man away from a life regulated by Christian standards and into the baseless moral confusion characterizing our age. Liberalism sought both to retain Christianity and to heed the most recent discoveries of science.

Liberalism in the Churches. Major Christian bodies soon found some of their leading men tilting toward liberal views. The preaching switched from a revivalistic emphasis on personal righteousness to a social gospel more interested in slum clearance. The Baptist, the Methodists, the Presbyterians—these churches witnessed the departure of groups who opposed the liberal drift of the parent bodies. In time Fundamentalism and Neo-Orthodoxy reacted, though in opposite directions. Pentecostalism was an indirect reaction, since believers here sought spiritual fulfillment outside the major bodies.

Doctrines

A technical analysis of the doctrinal defects of liberalism was written by Carl F. H. Henry and entitled *Remaking the Modern*

Mind.[5] Acknowledgement is made to that volume for the following list of liberal principles, though the wording here has been simplified.

The Bible is Fallible. Not infallible, as evangelicals conceive. Liberalism views the Bible as the product of men inspired as the great writers of all ages, yet still subject to error.

Man Is Basically Good. He is not a sinner, but he is "out of adjustment." This viewpoint has been forcibly modified by the testimony to the evil imaginations of man's heart rising from the smoke of two world wars in a single generation.

God Is Everybody's Father. "The universal fatherhood of God" —it is commonly expressed. But this confuses those who are God's sons by *creation* (everybody) with those who are His sons by *recreation* (John 1:12).

Nature Is Unbroken. Everything happens according to natural law. There is therefore nothing miraculous, nothing that suspends natural law. Accordingly, Christ's virgin birth and His resurrection are ruled out as historical events.

Progress Is Certain. The old liberals were optimistic: they were spurred by rapid scientific advance to believe in automatic progress. The world, they thought, was getting better and better day by day.

Evaluation

Liberalism of this type is losing ground. The events of the twentieth century have forced it to take more seriously the reality and deep-seated nature of sin. Since this is what the Bible says of human nature, the Bible is now given greater credence. The new science of Archaeology has made rapid strides in confirming the accuracy and reliability of the Bible. Liberalism is not dead, but it has been seriously wounded.

NEO-ORTHODOXY

Orthodoxy means correct doctrine. It refers to Bible believing, evangelical theology. The prefix *Neo-* means new. Neo-Orthodoxy therefore is a new stress on orthodoxy.

History

Lessons from History. Neo-Orthodoxy is essentially a reaction against the optimistic teaching of liberalism. This reaction arose

---

[5]Carl F. H. Henry, *Remaking the Modern Mind* (Grand Rapids: Wm. B. Eerdmans Publishing Company, 1946).

from the portrayal of the evil nature of man disclosed pathetically in the two world wars of our century. We need only think of the Nazi gas chambers and ovens in which six million Jews were exterminated to see that advancing science does not mean advancing morality. This stubborn fact embarrassed liberalism: as scientific achievements spiralled upward astronomically, human evil careened downward with astonishing definiteness.

Karl Barth. Born in 1886, this German pastor was trained as a liberal. He found it difficult to tell German widows that their husbands had been slaughtered in a horrible war conducted by men who were "basically good." He sought the truth, found it in the Bible—in Romans especially. In 1919 he published a commentary on Romans directed to his fellow liberals and telling them, in effect, that the War and Paul agreed: man, after all, is a sinner. From Barth came a theological revolution.

Doctrines

A movement as recent and as informal as Neo-Orthodoxy does not have a clear statement of beliefs. Yet there are widely held ideas:

Man Is a Sinner. This is taken at face value, and it clearly divides the Neo-Orthodox from the unrepentant liberal.

Reason Is Not Trustworthy. If man is a sinner, so is his reason. Neo-Orthodoxy says revelation is superior to reason—a statement rejected by liberals but accepted by evangelicals.

The Word of God Is Experience. God's Word is an event, an experience—by no means merely a book. It is this teaching which hinders acceptance of Neo-Orthodoxy as an evangelical movement. Denying the Bible an objective status as written-down revelation, Neo-Orthodoxy loses an outside test for valid religious experience.

Biblical Criticism Is Valid. Since the Bible, on Neo-Orthodox assumptions, is not the only Word of God, it does not hurt if attitudes toward its multiple composition are adopted in full. In fact, Neo-Orthodoxy thinks it has an even greater miracle to find an infallible God speaking through a fallible book.

Evaluation

Neo-Orthodoxy's stress of the reality of sin, its view of the exaltedness of God, its requirement of personally experienced revelation—these are all welcome truths. But the movement is open to criticism in its low view of the trustworthiness of the Bible, in its habit of attaching unorthodox meaning to orthodox terms, and in its disregard for logical soundness in doctrinal statement. It is, some evangelicals believe, a new form of modernism—reason's refusal to give place to the unchanging Word of God, the Bible.

For Further Reading

Primary sources for these groups are generally technical and difficult to understand, though the Unitarians can supply readable pamphlets. The following volumes are inexpensive paperback editions and will be of value and interest to the reader: J. I. Packer, *Fundamentalism and the Word of God* (Eerdmans, 1958); J. G. Machen, *Christianity and Liberalism* (Eerdmans, 1923): The core issue in these competitive interpretations of Christianity is the nature of Biblical authority. An informative yet readable introduction to this problem was written by Bernard Ramm and entitled *The Pattern of Religious Authority* (Eerdmans, 1957).

For Discussion

1. What is the fundamental trait of modernism?
2. How is this trait applied in each of the four groups here discussed?
3. What is good and what is bad about Neo-Orthodoxy?

CHAPTER XIII

Interpreting the Isms

We have viewed in order a vast parade of twenty movements each claiming to define the truth, none aligning precisely with evangelical Christianity. The many varied beliefs have been interesting: some are ridiculous, some are blasphemous, but some make us re-examine our own faith.

The many cults are like Joseph's many-colored coat. There are the brilliant hues of Mormonism's quaint frontier-fostered faith. There are the faded unidentifiable colors of mystical, Oriental-based teachings whose essence is evasive. There are the gloomy greys of annihilationism.

In the midst of such an array of competing claims to truth, how can we distinguish the single one that must be true—if there is any truth at all? Or shall we take the depressing view that there is no absolute truth, no sure and certain way, and, therefore, in the end no lasting assurance of having found the truth? Shall we always be seekers, never finding though always searching?

To this dim prospect the Bible speaks a resounding word of simple optimism: we can know the truth. It is an open secret. In fact the truth is not an "it" at all: it is a "He." For Jesus said simply, "*I* am the truth" (John 14:6). Other teachers would guide pupils to the right ideas leading to an understanding of the truth. But Jesus taught that the truth is a Person—Himself. Knowing the truth meant knowing Him. And that kind of knowledge did not depend on enlightened intelligence as the intellectual cults taught. This living knowledge comes in a simple relationship with a Person, with Jesus.

LESSONS TO LEARN

We could, if we wished, stop short with identifying the errors of the isms and providing an effective response to them. But it is possible to learn from an opponent. By disregarding for a moment the obvious defects of the cults, we can focus on certain lessons which they can teach us.

What are these lessons we learn from our unwitting teachers? We can learn about—

Communicating the Gospel

To what great and endless efforts the cults go in broadcasting their messages! Two magazines of the Jehovah's Witnesses exceed five million monthly copies—in more than 50 languages. The Baha'is circulate literature in 130 languages. It is a serious question whether there would be the menacing threat of the cults today were it not for their well-oiled printing presses. The Unitarians, with no aggressive literature program, have not grown significantly. The Jehovah's Witnesses with tons of free tracts and millions of fifty-cent, hard bound books are circling the globe, having won the banner of the "world's fastest growing religion."

Think about it: it is the religion that writes that wins. No insignificant part in the bounding growth of Roman Catholicism has been played by the propaganda efforts of the advertising Knights of Columbus.

From this, Christianity may be reminded of a lesson it periodically forgets: there is power in the written Word. God Himself put His Word in writing in the Bible. And then there is the lowly tract. Who can estimate the extent of its influence? We need a higher appreciation and an increased use of this useful instrument of evangelism.

There are other ways in which the cults get across their message. Christian Science uses the reading room. Unity gives you a phone number which you can call any time day or night and know that someone will be there to record your prayer request. Jehovah's Witnesses actually set their literature on street corners. Christian Science gives their literature away in bus and train stations and airline terminals, where stopovers present an opportune potential for random reading. Mormonism sends people to your door with a polite little "sermon" to "share" with you. Moral Re-Armament buys double-page spreads in *Time* magazine to make a mass presentation of its idea. Rosicrucianism advertises all over the publishing world. "Frank and Ernest" tell you the Dawn Bible Student truth over their chatty radio programs.

Are there unexplored ways in which the church may communicate the truth that is in Jesus?

The Nature of Error

"Many a heresy," said a recent theologian, "has ridden into history on the back of truth." The confusing thing about the cults is that they mingle truth with error. And the dividing lines are out of focus. We could set down basic truths of the Christian faith beside the cults which have carried that truth to an unallow- able extreme. For example:

Jehovah's Witnesses	Right will triumph in the future.
Christian Science	God's primary will is wholeness.
Spiritualism	There is a real unseen world.
Unitarianism	There is but one God.

Yet these same groups turn around and assert un-Biblical con- clusions:

Jehovah's Witnesses	Christ came in 1914.
Christian Science	There is no evil.
Spiritualism	We should communicate with departed spirits.
Unitarianism	God is not a Trinity.

If the cults were all error, the matter would be simplified. But they are a skillful mixture of truth and error. We need a revival of the spiritual gift of "discerning of spirits" spoken of in I Corin- thians 12:10.

The Subtlety of Satan

If all Satan's emissaries in the world today looked like the halloween suits supposed to represent the devil, there would be no problem in recognizing his work. But they do not. The horned, glowering devil with a pitchfork in his hand is no more than a cartoon. Satan comes as "an angel of light" (II Corinthi- ans 11:14). You have to recognize as you stand there talking to that manifestly sincere person so thoroughly and sacrificially com- mitted to his cult, that this is the way Satan works.

There may be people "possessed of the devil," whose eyes and voice have revealing signs. But Satan's usual device is the honest, upright cultist who nearly bowls you over with his sincerity, his honesty, his gentlemanliness, his high moral standards, his ab- solute unlikelihood of being a messenger of Satan. But he is —even though he does not know it. The serpent, remember, "was more subtile than any beast of the field" (Genesis 3:1). I am not saying every adherent of every cult or ism is thus an unwitting

apostle of Satan: I am saying that when one does appear, this is
the way he strikes us. Like Paul, we should not be ignorant of
Satan's devices (II Corinthians 2:11).

The Psychology of Belief

This may be tied in with the previous item. But it is astonishing
what people will believe. Anyone, it appears, can acquire a following if his doctrine is novel enough. The year 1844 dates the arrival
of Baha'u'llah for thousands of Baha'is but it marks a shift in
Christ's ministry for other thousands of Seventh-day Adventists.
Both use Daniel 8:14 as the prophetic starting point. As a Mormon, I would have to believe that God used to be like me and
that I one day shall be as He is.

People, it seems, have to believe something. Anything that
makes a whit of sense will gather dedicated disciples. Even if
it is only believing that there's nothing worth believing! For the
Christian, this spells opportunity: John wrote his entire Gospel
in order that people might believe (John 20:30, 31). And it is
just this belief in the Christian sense—its presence or its absence
—that fixes the great eternal gulf (John 3:36).

DANGERS TO AVOID

While we may pick up some good pointers from the cults,
we must not blind ourselves to their fundamental errors. Here
are three points of confusion within the cults.

Confusing What Man Does with What God Did

The correct theological word is *autosoterism*—self-salvation.
Says J. K. Van Baalen in his book *The Chaos of Cults*, ". . . there
are but two religions in the world. The one is autosoterism, that
salvation is from man. The other ascribes the entire work of
salvation from the world's ills to God."[1]

Christianity is based on *what God did* for mankind in giving
His Son at Calvary. The cults, indeed all religions apart from the
gospel of the grace of God, outline *what man must do*—and probably keep doing—to save himself. Christianity glories in a single
event accomplished in the past. Other religions go about doing
things by which they seek relief from guilt or entrance into some
higher life.

---

[1] J. K. Van Baalen, *The Chaos of Cults*, pp. 15, 16.

Confusing Human Goodness with Spiritual Righteousness

"All our righteousnesses are as filthy rags," was Isaiah's evaluation (Isaiah 64:6). "Not by works of righteousness which we have done," Paul explained to Pastor Titus, "but according to his mercy he saved us" (Titus 3:5). The good that men do—and they do a lot that is good—is approved by God. He desires men to do good. But all the good man can muster is still his own goodness. If our estimate of the reality of sin equals that of the Bible, we must see that such goodness is never good enough. And that is why God in Christ imparts to us His own goodness.

Spiritual righteousness is imputed: that is, it is written up to one's account when it really was not his own. God in Christ receives the sinner. He then looks on that sinner as He does on His own Son: for the sinner is now in that Son, "in Christ." It is then no longer human goodness that counts, but Christ's faultless righteousness. Christians periodically need to be reminded of this glorious gospel truth. There seems to be an inward tendency in man to do some kind of work by which he might merit God's favor. But the grace of God is precisely this—unmerited favor.

Human goodness is what God expects. But it is powerless to save. Spiritual righteousness is what God gives in crediting the perfect righteousness to the ledgers of all who believe He is gracious enough to do just that.

Confusing Intellectual with Experimental Knowledge

Many of the cults take a gnostic approach: they offer some "truth," which if perceived will become the key to life. Salvation, or its equivalent, becomes an intellectual matter. The more you know the better off you are eternally.

Christianity speaks of experimental knowledge—knowledge that is the result, not of an experiment, but of experience. Since Christians know the Truth to be a Person, the knowledge they speak of is personal acquaintance with that Person. Jesus Himself defined eternal life in terms of such personal, experimental knowledge: "And this is life eternal, that they might know thee the only true God, and Jesus Christ, whom thou has sent" (John 17:3). Such knowledge, unlike a discovered secret, is subject to growth as one person comes to know better the other Person. "But grow in grace, and in the knowledge of our Lord and Saviour Jesus Christ" (II Peter 3:18). Paul's prayer for the Colossians was, in part, "that ye might walk worthy of the Lord unto all pleasing, being fruitful in every good work, and increasing in the knowledge of God" (Colossians 1:10).

Paul's remark to the Corinthians suits the church today: "Awake to righteousness, and sin not; for some have not the knowledge of God: I speak this to your shame" (I Corinthians 15:34).

STEPS TO TAKE

We have taken a long look at the isms and the problem they present to the church. What shall we do about them as individual believers? How shall we adequately meet their challenge? Here are some concrete steps to take:

Personally Meet the Truth—Jesus Christ

Christ said, "I am the way, the truth, and the life" (John 14:6). No one comes to the Father except by Him. Whoever knows that the Truth is a Person can understand that personal relationships can become more personal, more intimate, just as you can come to know an acquaintance better through closer association. Surely the first thing to do in the light of the cults is to get to know Jesus Christ better. How can we do this? The Bible promises another Comforter whose very mission would be to glorify Jesus (John 14:16). He would receive the things of Jesus and pass them on to the disciples of Jesus. Being filled with the Spirit brings us into a closer relationship with the Lord Jesus.

Obey His Words

A number of the cults seek the *way* of Jesus but do not heed His *words*. The two—His way and His words—cannot be separated. "If a man love me," Jesus said, "he will keep my words: and my Father will love him, and we will come unto him, and make our abode with him" (John 14:23). "He that saith he abideth in him ought himself also so to walk, even as he walked" (I John 2:6). "And why call ye me, Lord, Lord, and do not the things which I say?" (Luke 6:46).

Obeying Jesus' words will result in accepting the teachings He gave. Mormonism's idea that the Father has flesh and bones crosses Jesus' words in John 4:24. The Christian Science denial of the reality of sin overlooks Jesus' words in John 8:7. The Jehovah's Witness rejection of the deity of Christ contradicts His own words in John 14:10.

Advice to follow the words of Jesus applies to the cults, but doubly so to the professing evangelical Christian.

Study the Bible

This is how we learn of the words of Christ. Whatever other literature is consulted in the attempt to learn about the cults, we cannot neglect the great sourcebook of the Christian faith. Here is the fountain of truth. The Bible is the Written Word as Christ is the Living Word. We know one and read the other, and our knowledge of each should deepen throughout the Christian life.

In this busy age, one way to guarantee a minimum program of Bible study is to follow regularly the Sunday school lessons, even though you are not called upon to teach. That way, you get into a portion of the Bible each week with a total balance achieved over the years.

Make good use of a concordance. Look up all the references to a single word that strikes you as you work with the Word. Try special studies. For example, in connection with your study of the cults read through the pastoral letters of Paul to Timothy and Titus and write down everything you find that speaks of doctrinal error and correctness, and anything else that impresses you as you think about what the pastoral letters say about the cults. You may be surprised at what you discover. Do not underestimate the possibilities of new insight coming afresh as you read God's Word.

Study Related Subjects

You have studied in this book a general survey of the cults. Pursue also a growing understanding of the history of the church. Delve into the area of Christian theology. Consider the study of apologetics—the defense of the Christian faith. Your pastor can supply suggestions for further reading along the lines of your own interest. The cults emphasize study. Should you do less?

Love People

Love is, as Henry Drummond entitled his little classic, "the greatest thing in the world." According to I Corinthians 13:13 love is more important that faith or hope—essential as they are. Love wins when nothing else will. We make it difficult, but each of us knows inside that he ought to love with more willingness and sacrifice. "Beloved, if God so loved us, we ought also to love one another" (I John 4:11). Try reading First John and underlining the word *love* every time it occurs.

Pray for the Cults

Pray that the true light of the gospel may shine in their seeking hearts. Pray for workers and methods effective in reaching them. God calls people as missionaries to Indian reservations; He calls some to special ministries, as to the deaf. Is it too much to expect that He will call some to specially effective ministries among the cults? Can there be missionaries who will be called to Salt Lake City or to Wilmette? We are to pray for harvesters, "but the laborers are few: pray ye therefore the Lord of the harvest, that he would send forth laborers unto his harvest" (Luke 10:2). This is a prayer for workers.

THE HEART OF THE GOSPEL

> I John 5:10–13. He that believeth on the Son of God hath the witness in himself: he that believeth not God hath made him a liar; because he believeth not the record that God gave of his Son. And this is the record, that God hath given to us eternal life, and this life is in his Son. He that hath the Son hath life; and he that hath not the Son of God hath not life. These things have I written unto you that believe on the name of the Son of God; that ye may know that ye have eternal life, and that ye may believe on the name of the Son of God.

The sole factor that determines a man's ultimate destiny is whether or not he "hath the Son"; whether or not he has believed in Jesus. This belief or its absence is known, in the final analysis, to God alone. It is the sole determining factor: the many other beliefs and forms of religions are secondary. That is why we leave to God the judgment of the cultist, for we are sure that "the Lord knoweth them that are his" (II Timothy 2:19). There is no doubt that many Seventh-day Adventists are good Christians. It may be there are other members of other cults, each of whom "hath the Son." If they do—and we leave that up to God who knows all things—they are saved apart from the teachings of their group.

So what is the heart of the gospel, its very core, its essential minimum? The answer can be suplied in three short statements:

1. *Sin Is Real*

Sin and evil are not imaginations of the mind, as Christian Science teaches. Sin is not a fairy tale, nor a myth, nor the mere "lack of adjustment." In the Biblical view it is a race-wide characteristic opposition to God, deep-seated in human nature, expressed in a multitude of sins, and correctable only by the forgiving grace of God and the sanctifying work of the Spirit of God (see Romans 3:23; 5:12–21).

2. *Salvation Is Complete*

Christ entered once for all into the presence of the Father with His eternal sacrifice of Himself (Hebrews 9:26). There remains nothing more that Almighty God can do to secure the redemption of mankind. He has given His only Son, He can do no more. The cults tend to leave salvation as an open-ended process, rather than as a completed and accomplished reality. But, thank God, the work is done.

3. *Belief Is Essential*

The Biblical idea of belief begins with the acceptance, mentally, of the truth of certain facts as factually accurate. But it does not stop there; it begins there. Belief in the Biblical sense means whole-hearted commitment of oneself—all he is and all he is not, just as he is—to Jesus Christ who demands that He be Lord of all. Belief becomes a process after this initial act of commitment—a process—of constant commitment, of little and big decisions—all made in the light of remaining steadfast in the love of God. As we keep ourselves in the love of God (Jude 21) we discover that we are kept by the power of God until the last day (I Peter 1:5).

For Discussion

1. Is it legitimate to learn anything from the cults and isms? Why?
2. How do the good works of Christians, which the Bible demands, relate to the spiritual righteousness credited to them through Christ?
3. How does Satan operate in the cults?
4. What is the very heart of the gospel?

A NOTE ON FURTHER READING

Suggested reading about the individual movements discussed in this book have been included at the close of each chapter. This will provide some guidance on books of a general, inclusive nature. Publisher and date are supplied for easy acquisition.

There are three works on the cults written from an evangelical point of view, each of which is a major review of the most significant cults. The oldest, the longest and the most widely known is J. K. Van Baalen's *The Chaos of Cults* (4th ed.; Eerdmans, 1962). The appendix of John Gerstner's book, *The Theology of the Major Sects* (Baker, 1960), incorporates very useful tables. One lists the cults, showing what each believes. Another lists areas of doctrine, showing what each cult says about that doctrine. It also includes a dictionary of terms used by the cults and a survey of the history and teaching of each.

The name of Walter R. Martin will be seen increasingly in the field of evangelical writing on the cults. His survey volume bears the title *The Rise of the Cults* (Zondervan, 1955). A more thorough analysis of all major cults has been planned for some years. When it appears, it will likely become the most authoritative book on the cults from an evangelical standpoint. In *The Christian and the Cults* (Zondervan, 1956) Dr. Martin presents useful information on a proper approach to the cults and assembles other information of interest. He has also written inexpensive pamphlets on Jehovah's Witnesses, Christian Science, Unity, and Mormonism which are the best of their kind, as well as reveal major studies of individual groups: *Jehovah of the Watchtower* (1953); *The Christian Science Myth* (1955) ; *The Truth about Seventh-day Adventism* (1960); and *The Maze of Mormonism* (1962)—all published by Zondervan.

Besides these evangelical volumes there are several books on the cults written by non-evangelicals. Their chief value lies in the historical facts they record. The best of these would include Marcus Bach, *They Have Found a Faith* (Bobbs-Merrill, 1951); Charles Braden, *These Also Believe* (Macmilliam, 1949); Charles Ferguson, *The Confusion of Tongues* (Doubleday, Doran, 1928); and more recently, Richard R. Mathison, *Faiths, Sects and Cults* (Bobbs-Merrill, 1960).

For statistics and addresses of headquarters offices one may consult the latest issue of the *World Almanac* or the *Yearbook of American Churches*—both standard references published yearly.

Frank Mead's *Handbook of Denominations* (Abingdon, 1960) is
not limited to the cults and is highly recommended for all teachers
and pastors and others interested in a quick-reference book where
the essential facts about the history, organization, doctrine, and
teachings of the major religious groups may be grasped in a few
moments.

Persons wishing to keep up with developments in the cults may
subscribe to the quarterly *Religious Research Digest*. This magazine is edited by Walter R. Martin, whose helpful works are mentioned above, and may be ordered at the current rate of two dollars
per year from the Christian Research Institute, 122 Beaufort
Avenue, Livingston, New Jersey. Religion Analysis Service, 902
Hennepin Avenue, Minneapolis, publishes *The Discerner*—"an
interdenominational heresy-exposing quarterly" at one dollar for
seven issues. They also will supply a catalog of tracts and pamphlets on the various cults.

Index

141

STATISTICS AND BELIEFS OF THE MAJOR CULTS

GROUP	CHAP-TER	STATISTICS		SOURCES OF AUTHO
		INCLUSIVE MEMBERSHIP	LOCAL CHURCHES	
Reference: EVANGELICAL CHRISTIANITY	–	National Association of Evangelicals enrolls 1.6 million, but serves 10 million. Thousands are in unaffiliated groups		The Bible
MORMONISM	II	1,647,546	4,398	The Bible; *The Book of M* *The Doctrine and Covenan* *The Pearl of a Great Price*
SEVENTH-DAY ADVENTISM	III	317,852	3,037	The Bible; Writings of Ellen G. White
SPIRITUALISM	IV	175,257	468	Revelations from the spir through mediums
CHRISTIAN SCIENCE	V	Prohibits reporting of statistics. Estimated membership 403,000		*Science and Health* and writings of Mary Baker E
JEHOVAH'S WITNESSES	VI	250,000	4,170	Writings of "Pastor" Russ Judge Rutherford
UNITY	VII	"My guess is that more than one third of denominationally identified Christians in the United States have read or are reading Unity material." – Marcus Bach		Writings of Charles and Fillmore
MORAL RE-ARMAMENT	VIII	(Not available)		Teachings of Frank Buchman
THEOSOPHY	IX	(Not available)		Tibetan "Mahatmas"; Writings of Helena P. Bla
BAHA'ISM	IX	Established in 5,000 localities in 255 countries		Writings of Baha'u'llah
ZEN BUDDHISM	IX	20,000	53	Writings of Gautama Budd
ROSICRUCIANISM	X	Estimated membership 45,000		Rosicrucian secrets
SWEDENBORGIANISM	X	5,875	68	Bible is "crown of reve Writings of Emanuel Swe
ROMAN CATHOLICISM	XI	42,104,900	23,393	The Church
HUMANISM	XII	(Not available)		Human reason
UNITARIANISM and UNIVERSALISM	XII	171,747	797	The free mind and the C tradition
LIBERALISM	XII	(Not available)		The free mind and the C tradition
NEO-ORTHODOXY	XII	(Not available)		"The Word of God" as a encounter

BELIEFS

THE GODHEAD	HUMAN NATURE AND SIN	WAY OF SALVATION	THE FUTURE
...tarian. Father, Son and Holy ...it – three distinct Persons ...are one in essence	Sin entered world through Adam's transgression; all men are by nature sinful	Man is saved by grace through faith in the vicarious atonement of the Lord Jesus Christ	Literal heaven for redeemed; literal hell for unredeemed
...Gods ...ather has a body of flesh ...bones	"What God is, man may become"	Found in the "restored church" founded by Joseph Smith	Three degrees of heaven
...dox	Orthodox	Legalistic	Millennium in heaven Annihilation of the wicked
...sonal principle	No Fall	Man is his own savior	No hell Spirit existence determined by life here
...sonal principle ...was a Christian Scientist ...Spirit is "divine science"	Sin and evil have no true existence	By understanding "divine science"	No hell All will eventually understand "divine science"
...ah alone is God ...is "God's chief Son"	All die for Adam's sin	Secured by Christ's ransom-death Second chance	Armageddon ahead, then the "New World" on earth
...sonal principle	Sin generally ignored	By self-improvement	Reincarnation
...dox	Deals primarily with committed sins; ignores origin of sin and the Fall	The Five C's International peace action	Not stressed
...sonal principle	Sin inevitable	Through meditation Repeated reincarnations permit perfection	Repeated reincarnations till soul loses consciousness
...is one, the same one wor-...ed by all religions	Sin is imperfection	Recognize relative nature of truth	Not stressed
...vine being known; this is ...ond human comprehension	Sin is wrong desire	The "eightfold path"	Nirvana
...tressed	Man capable of self-mastery	Mastering Rosicrucian secrets	Not stressed
...Father and the Spirit are ...ects of Christ	Sin is not transmitted	Salvation is not by faith alone	Judgment already past Second Coming occurred in arrival of Swedenborg's message
...dox	Orthodox	Found only in the Roman Catholic church	Generally orthodox, except for doctrine of purgatory
...s toward atheism	Vast potential in man	Scientific, cultural, technological advance	Further "evolution"
...ather alone is God ...a Great Teacher	Man basically good	Concerned self-improvement	Here and now of greater importance Future uncertain
...ound within the universe	Man basically good	Largely through collective social action	No literal hell Future uncertain
...is indefinable because He ...ifferent from all else that ...ts; Christ divine	Man basically evil	By "personal encounter" with God in Christ	Either orthodox or mythical

chart summarizes briefly the distinctive teachings of the groups discussed in this book. Astrology, Anglo-...ism, and Father Divine are omitted, since they major on one specific teaching and are not complete systems. ...ership statistics, which have been provided where applicable, have been drawn chiefly from the Yearbook ...erican Churches, 1962 Edition, edited by Benson Landis and published by the National Council of Churches. ...sources, however, have been used in some cases.